Ferrari 156
SHARKNOSE

Ferrari 156
SHARKNOSE

Ed McDonough

Foreword by Phil Hill

SUTTON PUBLISHING

For David Hodges and Bill Butcher

First Published in 2001 by
Sutton Publishing Limited · Phoenix Mill
Thrupp · Stroud · Gloucestershire ·GL5 2BU

Reprinted in 2002

British Library Cataloguing in Publication Data
A catalogue record for this book is available from the British Library

ISBN 0 7509 2731 3

Half-title page: Phil Hill, Monaco, 1961. (Jim Gleave/Atlantic Art)
Title page: Phil Hill, Wolfgang von Trips, Richie Ginther, French Grand Prix, 1961. (Ferrari Centro Documentazione)
Front endpaper: Just after the start of the French Grand Prix, 1961. (Author's Collection)
Back endpaper: Willy Mairesse leading Stirling Moss, Brussels Grand Prix, 1962. (Author's Collection0

Typeset in 10.5/13.5 Photina.
Typesetting and origination by
Sutton Publishing Limited.
Printed and bound in England by
J.H. Haynes & Co. Ltd, Sparkford.

CONTENTS

FOREWORD

by Phil Hill, 1961 World Champion

Winning the Italian Grand Prix for Ferrari in 1960 was very special for me, as an American hadn't won a Grand Prix for thirty-nine years. Enzo Ferrari had been developing a new, rear-engined car for the new regulations set to come into effect in 1961. Many of the teams were dead set against the new formula, but the first signs were that the 156 Ferrari was going to be a strong contender in 1961.

I also had the feeling that 1961 could be a very good year for the Ferrari team and for me, but it turned out to be a very difficult season. To the outside world it must have looked as if the 'Sharknose' Ferrari was unbeatable, but from the inside it was very different. Enzo Ferrari never declared who was to be the team's number one driver, which kept Wolfgang von Trips and me on edge all season. There was always an uncomfortable feeling in the team, and while the car was very competitive, I never was convinced that the Championship was going to be easy or even possible to win. Ferrari politics were always present in a way that did not make life comfortable for the drivers or others in the team.

Nevertheless, those were very special days in racing, and 1961 and 1962 saw some great races. I certainly had some good days and some bad ones too. Now that it is forty years since I won the World Championship, it is especially interesting to look back at how different the racing scene and the people were then. The whole approach to Grand Prix racing was very different. Though the politics don't always change, the sport certainly has.

This book has managed to capture the flavour and the context of a period which

Opposite: In practice at the 1961 Italian Grand Prix Hill tows Ginther and Rodriguez, with Brabham and von Trips just behind coming off the banking. (Archive von Trips/Födisch) *Below:* Phil Hill. (Graeme Simpson/Motor Racing Tradition)

won't come again. The 'Sharknose' Ferrari was a special car and I think Ed McDonough has managed to draw an accurate picture of a particular stage of motor racing history by concentrating on one very special and successful racing car from that time. It was an epoque of larger than life characters, people like Carlo Chiti who played such an important role at Ferrari though perhaps he was overshadowed by Enzo Ferrari himself. There were also von Trips, Richie Ginther, Stirling Moss and Jim Clark, some of the truly talented drivers. Racing was full of great characters then. Those years were a kind of rollercoaster of highs and lows, but they do manage to stand out as special times.

Phil Hill

INTRODUCTION

Any serious motorsport enthusiast has a certain number of 'defining' moments, occasions you can recall many years later and that, in some way, influenced or possibly drastically changed your life. This author had two distinct defining moments. The first occurred in the basement of the family house in Stamford, Connecticut, where as a twelve-year-old I rummaged through a growing collection of *Hot Rod* and *Motor Trend* magazines. Though this was late in 1953, the *Motor Trend* report of the 1953 Mille Miglia read like something which had happened just minutes ago, or at least it did to that car-smitten youth, and the name Fangio entered an early cerebral database which was to grow forever.

Fangio had completed the Mille Miglia in his Alfa Romeo 6C 3000CM, or Disco Volante as it was known then – inaccurately, as I would learn later. The car bore some resemblance to Alfa Romeo's original 1952 prototype sports model, the C-52, which actually looked like a wheeled flying saucer, and anything resembling flying saucers in those days caught the attention of an eager and paranoid public, never mind an impressionable motor-oriented youth. Fangio had led the Mille Miglia and was on his way to victory when a collapsed steering arm meant he was left with control of only one front wheel, yet he drove the last 100 miles at a virtually unabated pace. Though overtaken by the eventual winner, Giannino Marzotto, Fangio had raised his world champion Grand Prix driver profile to that of generic hero for millions.

For this author he planted the seed of motor racing passion, and established something just short of fanaticism for Italian cars, especially Alfa Romeo at first, but this rapidly spread to cover the spectrum. Within days I had purchased my first plastic Ferrari kit, a 166 Barchetta. The racing bug had bitten, though it remained unfocused and included the early days of Bonneville, custom cars and hot rods, Indy cars, and sprint cars at the Danbury State Fairgrounds.

The second 'moment' came in early adult days, on a Sunday in September 1961: Count Wolfgang von Trips and a number of spectators had died at the Italian Grand Prix when his Ferrari 156 – the car known as the 'sharknose' – crashed. The image of the flared nose of the Ferrari 156 churning through a mass of helpless spectators was both morbid and irresistible; the man who was about to become world champion was dead. Though Trips might well have been the model hero for an aspiring though unlikely future racing driver, it wasn't Trips who got logged into that perpetual inner database, but the car. This small-engined antithesis to the American 'big banger' atmosphere the author had grown up in was the most perfect and beautiful expression of a true racing machine. It was aesthetically flawless in its styling and presentation; it was absolutely the right vehicle for an heroic racing driver. That Trips's death, to young and unsophisticated eyes, allowed the championship to go to an American also driving a 156, the first to take those laurels, was just another indication that the car could do anything.

That callow twenty-year-old didn't go out and become an instant success on the race tracks of the world, nor did he find an old 'sharknose' to treasure, but he did become hooked on the story, the period and the people. He didn't dream then that not quite forty years later he would be talking to that same world champion about that same Ferrari. The impact just never wore off.

Phil Hill became 1961 World Champion driver, von Trips passed into legend, Ferrari won its first constructors' title, an award instituted in 1958 which has become as important as the drivers' championship, too important in the view of many in modern-day motor racing. The Ferrari 156 seemed invincible to the world at large, but as quickly as its star rose in 1961, it fell again in 1962, a fairly dismal season where Hill, try as he might, couldn't retain his title and neither could Ferrari. The car that had swept to victory with apparent ease the previous year couldn't keep up with the mainly British-built opposition.

This book tries to unravel the story of those two fascinating years, the tale of the rise to bittersweet glory and the fall. It describes the intricacies of an era of motor racing where one car and constructor emerged above the rest in a time of turmoil and unwanted regulations. While the Ferrari 'sharknose' has been described and written about in almost every book on Ferrari and in every race report of the time, the author's own long-standing fascination with the car, the men who drove it, their opponents and teams – indeed, the whole feel of the period – has fostered the desire to explore that short era in depth.

Derek Hill, son of World Champion Phil, himself an accomplished and able racing driver, told the author at Goodwood how the Ferrari 'sharknose' achieved the status of an icon in his life. While the Hill home was not full of 1961 memorabilia, Derek grew up aware of the significance of the car to his father, and its beauty as an F1 machine had its own impact on Derek himself.

This, then, is the story of where the 156 came from, how it developed, who raced in it and against it, who was involved in its brief career. While it has become fashionable for many authors to put in a disclaimer at this point and say this book is not a 're-hash' of old race reports, this author takes a different line. The races of the time were the testing ground for Grand Prix cars, as well as providing a social arena for the drivers. The real drama was in the races. So this book looks at every race and every driver who raced the 'sharknose' and at a number of the 156's opponents, but it uses the words of several of the combatants of the time to reveal details of the story. It puts one contemporary Formula 1 car and team in perspective without glossing over the thorny elements and bitter struggles of the 'Sharknose's' history.

Wolfgang von Trips (left) and
Ferrari team-mate Phil Hill.
(Archive von Trips/Fodisch)

The author may have started as a Ferrari-loving wide-eyed enthusiast,
but he has, hopefully, become realistic and accurate in telling the not-
always-pleasant tale. In the main this book aims to be a vivid portrait of
another time, not that long ago in years, but now distant from modern
Grand Prix racing. While politics are today no stranger to Formula 1, the
drivers and the cars are totally different, and the last vestiges of a sport
are gone and Grand Prix racing has become a business. This author
preferred then to now and attempts to draw a picture of why he feels this
way. All the bias expressed in this story is the author's, except when those
who kindly contributed allow theirs to be included as well!

The errors, alas, are the author's alone. Every attempt has been made
to cross-check details and not repeat too many of the mistakes often
passed down from one writer to another. In relation to chassis numbers,
as much care as possible has been taken to be accurate in this area. None
of the author's predecessors were particularly clear where this
information came from. This author has consulted the records of John
Godfrey and his notes from Stanley Nowak, and these generally
correspond with the work of others.

The author is greatly indebted to a number of people who contributed
not only to this book, but to the story of the Ferrari 156 'sharknose' and its
time. Thanks are due in great measure to those who agreed to be
interviewed for this book: Phil Hill, Stirling Moss, John Surtees, Cliff Allison,
Rob Walker, Maurice Trintignant, Roy Salvadori, Trevor Taylor, John
Cooper, Tim Parnell, Tony Brooks, Jack Brabham, Cedric Selzer, Sally Stokes
Swart and Derek Hill. The only regret is that there wasn't time and space to

Wolfgang von Trips. (Archive von Trips/Fodisch)

talk to every other surviving driver and witness to the races of those years.

Additional thanks are due to Dan Gurney, first for supplying some key information at short notice, and secondly for being the kind of person who makes writing such a book a great pleasure, Gurney also has a link to the 'defining moments'. In 1964, when my daughter was two and was asked what she wanted for Christmas, she answered: 'Dan Gurney'. Such was her sad life at age two! In 1998 I told Dan this story and he promptly picked up the phone, called Heather, then thirty-six, and said: 'This is Santa Claus . . . I'm sorry I'm so late getting in touch.'

The majority of pictures included here have never been published. The author is grateful for all the help received in finding interesting photographs without having to make use of the usual commercial sources and libraries. Particular thanks are due to Jim Gleave/Atlantic Art for access to his superb collection, to Brian Joscelyn, John Blunsden, Ted (Ferret Fotographics) Walker, Graeme Simpson/Motor Racing Tradition, Tim Watson and Ferrari SpA, to Joan Godfrey for the loan of photos from the collection of the late John Godfrey, Paul Meis, Michael Lindsay, Jerry Sloniger, Jorg-Thomas Fodisch and Trips-Sportstiftung/Fodisch, Raymond Jenkins, Graham White, James Beckett and the BRDC Archives, Eric Sawyer, Eoin Young and Terry Hoyle and to Martin Hadwen and the BRSCC/*Motor Racing* Archives. Thanks also go to Graham Gauld for his pictures and long-standing encouragement to write.

There is another group of people who need to be thanked for their contributions which came in a variety of ways, and perhaps some of them should also be blamed, for they are in part responsible for my writing this book. They include von Trips and Fangio for starting it all, and Phil Hill for keeping it going for so long, and especially Phil Hill for always being so thoughtful and inquisitive about racing, thus providing a model for serious scrutiny of motor racing history.

The author holds Mike Lawrence, motorsport journalist and Shakespearean expert, responsible for the sometimes personal style of writing and the decision not always to take a popular view on some aspects of the subject. Mike has taught me to say what I think and write about it. I also blame the late and much missed David Hodges for providing a model of dedication to one's subject over a lifetime, though I can't live up to his example. Denis Jenkinson has to come in for his share of the blame as well, but mainly he must be thanked for the wonderful record of racing that he kept and wrote down, as well as for his fastidious approach to gathering details. Then I must thank my colleague in Italian car and racing mania, Peter Collins, for his endless supply of material and encouragement, and Casey Annis for allowing me to put off other jobs in order to finish this one! And finally Nancy, who has had to put up with this for forty-two years.

PRELUDE TO A CHAMPIONSHIP

Where did the Ferrari 'sharknose' come from? That question has several possible answers: one in respect of Ferrari's longer-term traditions, one in relation to the changes taking place in motor sport at the time, and at least one related to the people who were at Ferrari in 1960, mainly Carlo Chiti.

The long-standing tradition at Ferrari was to concentrate attention on what Enzo Ferrari considered to be the heart of the car, the engine. From his pre-war days running the racing team at Alfa Romeo at least through the 1960s, Enzo Ferrari was sometimes seen as being almost obsessed with engine development rather than chassis improvement or changes in the way brakes could be used, hence the fairly long delay in adopting disc brakes. While much of Ferrari's public oratory was part of his theatrical style as a car manufacturer, and he liked the sound of his own voice especially when making proclamations, he did indeed believe whole-heartedly in engine development, and thus the company produced some of the finest road and track engines of all time.

Another long-held belief at Ferrari was that the engine belonged in the front, something that very few racing car builders disagreed with until the late 1950s. This tradition persisted in spite of the enormous success of the pre-war Auto Unions, which often seem to have lost the credit for winning Grand Prix races with a mid- or rear-engined car. Quality engine development in a chassis designed to take the powerplant in the front was the life-long work of Vittorio Jano. As early as the 1920s he was known to Enzo Ferrari, who had a role in poaching the diminutive engineer from Fiat to Alfa Romeo. Jano then moved to Lancia in 1937 and spent years developing and improving a double overhead camshaft six-cylinder Lancia racing engine, as well as the potent V8 which powered the Lancia D-50 F1 car in the mid-1950s. When Lancia dropped out of competition and Ferrari took over the racing equipment and cars, he also obtained the services of Jano, by this time a design consultant. At Ferrari, Jano set to work in building a V6 for racing. One of his first projects was to create something for the then Formula 2, which had a 1500cc capacity limit.

Most of the biographies of Enzo Ferrari make considerable reference to his son Alfredo 'Dino' Ferrari, born in 1932, who was never healthy, either as a child or as a young man. He went to work at the factory and was credited, especially in books and articles in which his father had a hand, with being the creator of a number of Ferrari engines and bodies. He was thought to have completed a correspondence course at the University of Fribourg in Switzerland and written a thesis on the design of the 1.5-litre four-cylinder engine. Later investigations failed to find any Ferrari on the register at Fribourg or at any other similar school during the period. Dino died at the age of twenty-four in 1956 from what has been variously described as leukemia or muscular dystrophy – the real cause of his life-long ill-health has been debated for some years. Enzo Ferrari's response to his son's death was to insist that all V6 and V8 engine creations should be called Dinos – slightly odd if Dino had in fact been interested in four-cylinder engines. The reality is that Dino Ferrari worked on some projects with designer Aurelio Lampredi and then with Jano when he came to Ferrari, and no doubt played some part in the six-cylinder racing engine project, but his involvement probably did not go much beyond that. However, his name became synonymous with a wide range of very successful racing cars. By the end of 1956 there were several variations of Jano's V6 up and running, with the same type of Lancia-inspired valve operation and the same cylinder heads, though with differing capacities and block sizes. These V6s could be divided into three groups: those with small block engines from 1.5 to 2 litres, medium 2.2 to 2.5 and large blocks of 2.9 to 3.2 litres. These units formed the bases for the Ferrari F1 and F2 cars from 1957 to 1960, and later would be adapted for yet another range, the 1961–2 Grand Prix cars. Interestingly, the first of the V6 engines was a 1.5-litre design nominally dubbed the 156.

This 1.5-litre engine would be used for Ferrari's attack on Formula 2 in 1957, and Jano refined his engine, choosing a 65-degree angle between the banks of the engine to accommodate the dohc layout and car-burettors. With the banks lined up in parallel, there was limited room for ducting, unlike in the V12s which had the two banks staggered with one ahead of the other. The bore and stroke of 70×64.5mm gave a capacity of 1489.35cc. and the engine produced 180bhp at 9000rpm, substantially ahead of the four-cylinder unit Coventry-Climax was building at the time. This engine was fitted into a tubular chassis that was in effect a scaled-down version of the Ferrari 801, which was what Ferrari was now calling the Lancia D-50 it had inherited. The completed car was referred to as the Dino 156. At the Naples Grand Prix in April 1957, Luigi Musso finished third in this F2 entry while the F1 cars took outright victory. Later in the season, Maurice Trintignant took first place in the Rheims F2 event that was on the bill with the French Grand Prix, beating all the Coopers.

This particular chassis, 0011, was used for occasional races over the next two years, Phil Hill driving it in the mixed F1/F2 grid at the German Grand Prix in August 1958. As the older style drum brakes started to fade, Hill slowed down but spun on oil and bounced off the hedges of the Nürburgring; despite this, he managed to finish fifth in class and ninth overall. After races at Siracusa and Monaco in 1959, the chassis was substantially revised in 1960 and won in the hands of von Trips at Siracusa after Stirling Moss's Porsche broke down.

During this same period – between 1957 and 1960 – Jano's 2.4-litre unit, the medium block, had been developed extensively and was fitted in the 246 F1 Dino, proving to be one of Ferrari's most powerful and reliable engines. But as 1959 arrived, front-engined victories in Grand Prix racing were becoming fewer, as first Cooper and then eventually Lotus began to point the way to the future with rear-engined machines.

It was at the end of the 1958 season that external forces began to shape the way Grand Prix racing would go for the next several years. On 29 October, the Royal Automobile Club in Pall Mall, London, witnessed a glittering event to honour the British World Champion, Mike Hawthorn and the British winner of the Constructors' Award, Vanwall, which had taken six Grand Prix events during the season. The evening was primarily a social and festive occasion, with some business thrown in at the end. When Commission Sportive Internationale (CSI) President, Auguste Perouse, came to the microphone, no one present could have known what was coming.

Perouse announced the regulations that would come into effect in 1961. Though this was still more than two years in the future, the announcement had an immediate and stunning impact. The new rules meant that Formula 1 cars would have engines with a cylinder capacity from 1300cc to 1500cc un-supercharged, and would run on com-

'Commendatore' Enzo Ferrari. (Alfa Romeo Centro Documentazione)

mercially available fuel. Furthermore, the cars would have a 500kg minimum weight limit, a protective roll-over bar, a double braking system, a self-starter, safety fuel tanks, and no oil was to be added during races. These rules would run from 1961 to 1965. The CSI Committee of seven members had voted 5–2 in favour, the two dissenters being the British and the Italian delegates. There was some irony in this in view of what would happen over the next few years.

A counter-formula was proposed, mainly under British influence, that would continue the life of the 2.5-litre cars and also include engines up to 3 litres. British support for this alternative was so strong that for some time the constructors, the drivers and the press all seemed to believe that the 'Inter-Continental Formula' would push the CSI regulations aside, or at least provide a viable alternative to the new rules.

In early 1959, Enzo Ferrari had made a public denial that he was planning a car with a rear- or mid-engine layout. This was revised to a statement that there were no 'immediate' plans for such a car, and at that stage 'immediate' must have meant the next day, because it was literally only forty-eight hours afterwards that, as Carlo Chiti, the senior competition engineer, later admitted, the rudimentary rear-engined chassis was sitting on the bench. Although von Trips had managed to beat Moss in that Siracusa race in early 1960, Chiti was well aware that the engine was no longer strong enough to dominate the 1500cc opposition, or at least not in the front-engined chassis. The engine in von Trips's car for that Siracusa race was a much-revised version of Jano's original which had been based on the small capacity block. Chiti was looking towards the future and wanted to develop something that would suit the range of cars Ferrari was likely to build in the next few years. Thus he decided to take Jano's medium-sized block, which had been used for the 246 F1 car, and revise it. This block could be used for the 2.4 engine but it could also be linered down and stroked so that it would not only suit F2 in 1960, but would also be something that could evolve into an F1 car in 1961, as both the 1960 F2 and 1961 F1 rules were limited to 1.5 litres. This revised 65-degree engine now had a bore and stroke of 73×58.8mm and a capacity of 1476cc, and ran with 38mm Weber carburettors to produce a reliable 180bhp. Chiti had also been planning an engine with a 120-degree angle between the banks, and knew that the same medium block could accommodate such a design, and that both the 65-degree unit and an eventual 120-degree engine would fit into the same chassis with relatively little difficulty.

Carlo Chiti was still only thirty-five at the end of 1959, and his design ideas were quick in coming. The plump graduate of the University of Pisa, where he had studied aeronautical engineering, arrived at Ferrari in 1957. It wasn't an easy time for a Tuscan's ideas to be accepted among the Modenese, but his introduction of independent rear suspension on the 246 Dino F1 car set the seal on his position. He was immensely inventive, and like many of his colleagues – for example, Jano – he was a tireless and devoted worker. His sense of timing was central to getting Enzo Ferrari to push forward with the development of the revised 1.5-litre 65-degree engine in late 1959. That opened the door: in March 1960, when it was clear that the engine alone wasn't enough to beat the rear-engined cars from Cooper and Porsche, Chiti was able to convince Ferrari to try a chassis with the engine behind the driver.

Chiti waited for the right moment to do this, and had even bought an F1 Cooper chassis from Scuderia Centro Sud to study how he would go about putting the Ferrari engine in the car. Work on this project progressed so swiftly that Chiti had the car ready for testing on 22 May at the Modena Autodrome, but it was fitted with one of the 246 Dino engines. As these engines were about to become surplus, Chiti intended to use them to test the chassis, and to modify them for the 1.5-litre car. If the tests went well, Ferrari would enter this design at Monaco with the 2.4 engine.

Ferrari test driver Martino Severi tried the car first, with its double-tube space frame and double-wishbone independent suspension. It had a bulbous and rather ungainly-looking body but the testing was successful, and during the tests Phil Hill had an opportunity to drive a rear-engined car for the first time. Severi tried a number of standing starts and no problems arose from hard use of the clutch. It was a smooth-looking car with a relatively low frontal area, and the feeling on the day was that it was aerodynamically more advanced than the front-engined 246. Hill did a number of back-to-back tests with a front-engined car to compare the two. Enzo Ferrari, in his grey suit, and Carlo Chiti in his shirt sleeves stood out on the corners, leaning forwards to get a closer look at Severi in this revolutionary car.

During this early period, Cliff Allison, who had driven the Lotus 12 several times in Grand Prix races of 1958 with a couple of good results, as well as taking the wheel of the Lotus 16 and a Maserati 250F, had joined Ferrari in 1959. He was one of the early testers of the rear-engined prototype. At Coys Festival in 2000 he spoke to the author:

Well, I drove it at Modena in the early days and I wasn't all that impressed at first. The surface at Modena, which is right in the town, is very bumpy and you had to know where all the holes were to go very quickly around it. I had an interesting experience there because when I joined Ferrari they were using the leaf-spring cars that Collins and Hawthorn drove in 1958. In 1959 Tony Brooks and I drove for them and we went out there to Modena to test them. They had these long leaf springs on them to start and when we came to drive the thing it was like driving an old American car – or bus! But they wouldn't change to coils until we went faster around Modena than the leaf-spring car. Well, the test driver they had, Severi, knew the track like the back of his hand, and he was going around in the leaf-spring car and Tony and I were going around in the coil-spring car, and we eventually did go faster. They changed to coils, but that was late in the day. The

Martino Severi tests the 1960 prototype at Modena on 22 May. (Graham Gauld)

Phil Hill in early tests of the 156 rear-engined prototype at Modena, 22 May 1960. (Graham Gauld)

Opposite: Von Trips before the start of the Solitude Grand Prix in Germany on 24 July 1960, his first race in the revised rear-engined prototype, chassis 0008. (Archive von Trips/Fodisch)

others had changed years ago. When it came to testing the rear-engined car, it was really set up for Ginther who was quite a small chap and I wasn't very comfortable in it. It didn't have a shark nose then, and I never tested it except in the way it ran in 1960. It was unfortunate for me having the accident I had at Monaco that year because Taffy and Phil and I were all driving pretty competitively at the time, and I was just as quick as they were, so it might have all been different. When I had that accident, Ferrari offered me a contract to drive again though not Formula 1, but to drive sports cars until I became qualified enough in his eyes to drive in Formula 1. Really I wish now I had done that but at that time I thought I had to be in Formula 1 because it was the only thing that had any money in it – and not a lot at that. If I had done that I probably would have gotten back into the team for 1961 or 1962.

It was Ferrari himself who made the decision to have Richie Ginther drive the car in the Monaco Grand Prix one week after the Modena testing. Chiti had wanted the new vehicle in the experienced hands of either Hill or von Trips. The car broke a drive shaft in practice and finished sixth. This was not a bad performance for a brand new design departing so much from tradition, but the car was many laps down and the Italian papers were very critical. Ferrari passed this criticism back to Chiti, who shelved the car, chassis 0008, at least as far as using it again to race with the 246 engine. Nevertheless Phil Hill tried it out again a week later in one of the practice sessions for the Dutch Grand Prix where,

on a circuit more suited to it, Hill was impressed with the way it handled, and began to realise how important the move to a rear-engined format would be. He was, however, to secure the last win for a front-engined Ferrari Grand Prix car in his great victory at Monza later in the year.

In July, Chiti had his way and put von Trips in the car for the F2 race at Solitude, near Stuttgart. The suspension had been improved and as a result of intensive work the body was now lower and altogether more striking. While Hill put the front-engined car on row 5, von Trips was at the front, next to pole-position man Jim Clark in his Lotus 18. In the wet practice, von Trips was a huge 30 seconds quicker than the rest. In the race, in front of nearly 200,000 spectators, Hans Hermann led most of the way after an initial battle between nine cars. Then von Trips fought all the way with Hermann's Porsche, got ahead in the last laps and went on to a rapturous win. Shortly afterwards, Ferrari gave Chiti a free hand in developing both single-seaters and sports cars, and finally accepted that the rear engined car was here to stay.

0008 came out twice more at the end of 1960, first for the Italian Grand Prix at Monza, where it had been decided to run von Trips with the 1.5-litre engine in the hope that it would get towed along by its bigger, front-engined team-mates. This duly happened, and it was Willy Mairesse who towed von Trips. A pit stop to check his tyres meant he dropped to fifth place (though first in the F2 class), thus ruining Ferrari's chance of a 1–2–3–4 finish. Still it was a fine result on the fast circuit. For Monza, the car had been tested thoroughly by Ginther and von Trips, and the rear hub carriers had been redesigned and cast in light alloy. The front suspension had also been changed, with the wishbones now angled downward towards the centre line of the frame in order to raise the front roll centre. Negative camber had now been achieved throughout the wheels' vertical travel. Several new pick-up points for the rear suspension had been drilled to broaden the range of adjustment. Chiti had always been enthusiastic about the importance of suspension geometry and was influenced by the British cars when he designed in so much negative camber. This would come back to haunt the team.

The German von Trips was out in the car again on 2 October for the Modena Grand Prix, an F2 race, where he followed Bonnier in the winning Porsche and Ginther's front-engined F2 156 across the line to third.

So as the end of 1960 approached, and the end of the 2.5-litre rules for F1 with it, the stalwarts at Ferrari were looking to Phil Hill and Wolfgang von Trips as the main driving strength, with Ginther doing testing and some racing.

Phil Hill, now thirty-two, had first met Enzo Ferrari in 1953 while he was driving with Luigi Chinetti at the Rheims 12-Hour sports car race. He was signed by Ferrari in 1954, and drove several times at Le Mans, winning for the first time in 1958. It was some time before Ferrari would let him graduate to Formula 1 and then he performed well in that division. Hill had been known for his direct, thoughtful and out-spoken approach. He always considered that he put his best into his driving but that there were many times when the best wasn't provided for him and by

Above: Von Trips leads Hans Herrmann's Porsche, Jim Clark's Lotus 18 and Bonnier's Porsche at Solitude, 1960. *Below*: Von Trips just before he took victory at Solitude. (Archive von Trips/Fodisch)

Above: The drivers' briefing before the Modena Grand Prix on 2 October 1960. Left to right: Huschke von Hanstein, Porsche team manager (in hat), Stirling Moss, Richie Ginther, Wolfgang von Trips. (Archive von Trips/Fodisch) *Below:* Phil Hill takes victory in the 1960 Italian Grand Prix at Monza, the last Grand Prix won by a front-engined car. (Raymond Jenkins)

Phil Hill at the end of the 1960 season. (Archive von Trips/Fodisch)

the time 1961 came around, he was part of the political fabric at Ferrari. There had even been some rumours that Graham Hill might have been approached to drive at the end of the 1960 season.

Wolfgang von Trips, known to his friends and associates as Taffy, had been in Grand Prix cars with Ferrari from 1956, and had also driven Ferrari sports cars and Porsches for a number of years. Enzo Ferrari was openly fond of von Trips, partly because of what he saw as his ability, but also because he was a baron and came from a very wealthy aristocratic

German family. This pedigree was something von Trips rarely made a fuss about, but it seems that Ferrari was impressed by it. While he was undoubtedly quick, he didn't have Hill's technical ability and knowledge. According to an apocryphal tale about von Trips's technical know-how, he was told the rear roll-bar was broken. He looked up over his shoulder at the roll-over hoop and is said to have replied: 'It looks OK to me.'

Richie Ginther, an American like Hill, with similar racing and mechanical background, came to Ferrari in 1960. He was always a popular man with his team-mates, at Ferrari and elsewhere, and, more than anyone else except Chiti, he contributed to making the rear-engined car a success from the beginning. He was one of the best test drivers of the period. He was fortunate that somehow he had not been in the team long enough to get swamped by company politics, and he remained free of this intrigue throughout his stay.

Romulo Tavoni had been at Ferrari for many years when he was appointed Team Manager for 1961. He had always been Enzo Ferrari's eyes and ears on the race scene and reported back after every event. The new job was to be difficult for him, because it meant he was responsible both to Ferrari and to the team itself for all the organisation of the F1 and sports car racing, and his loyalties were often divided. Fortunately, he was well liked by the drivers and by *Ingegnere* Chiti who knew what Tavoni was up against.

1961
THE SEASON STARTS

Who was Giancarlo Baghetti? At the age of twenty-six and a few months, the wealthy young Milanese gave Ferrari the first victory for the 156 in its 'shark-nose' mode, and the scene was set for the 1961 Formula 1 season. Baghetti had a rapid though not particularly sensational rise to fame. He had had his first racing competition only recently in 1958, when he and his brother Marco had managed to 'borrow' their father's Alfa Romeo 1900 Sprint which they tuned and ran in the 1958 version of the Mille Miglia. This race had been emasculated into a rally following the disastrous accident that cost the life of Alfonso de Portago, his co-driver and many spectators the previous year. The pair finished second and Giancarlo's secret didn't remain secret very long – it had been intended that he would join the family's business, Acorso Baghetti, which produced a wide range of metal products for industry in the north of Italy, but young Baghetti was intent on a career in motor racing.

Carlo Abarth took Baghetti on to race the 750 'double-bubble' Fiat-Abarth Zagato, and he drove several races in an Alfa Romeo Giulia Ti in 1959. Angelo Dagrada, a friend of Baghetti and his brother, had tuned the Alfa 1900 for the Mille Miglia Rally and was developing a front-engined Formula Junior to carry his own name in the new international junior single-seater category. Baghetti bought Dagrada's first car to contest the Italian championship in 1960, taking the rather basic design with its Lancia V4 engine and off-set suspension to several wins, seconds and thirds – enough, in fact, to gain him the Italian championship before the hordes of Lotus 18s and other British-built machines took over the category for good. The Dagrada was reliable as well as moderately quick in Baghetti's hands (that same car is still racing and appeared at the Monaco Historics in 2000).

Baghetti's record in Formula Junior brought him to the attention of Eugenio Dragoni and, as Graham Gauld tells the tale after interviewing Baghetti a few years ago, shortly before his untimely death from cancer, Dragoni drove Giancarlo to meet Enzo Ferrari in early December 1960. In what started out as a casual conversation, Dragoni decreed that Baghetti should drive in Formula 1 in 1960. What Baghetti took to be a joke became reality when Signor Ferrari simply stated he should join the F1 team in 1961, albeit on a 'restricted basis', which meant he wouldn't have a contract and wouldn't drive in all the races. For Baghetti, who was skilful but had come from nowhere, this was virtually unbelievable. The reality that put Baghetti in the seat of a Formula 1 Ferrari for the first time was a combination of Dragoni's forceful manner and the fortunate coincidence that there was a way in which Italian drivers could get some Formula 1 experience without a manufacturer risking too much embarrassment by having him in a works team.

First Dragoni got Baghetti several days' practice at Monza in a 250 GT Ferrari SWB, in which the rising star set impressive times and lowered the existing GT record by some 4 seconds. Dragoni's Scuderia Sant Ambroeus was one of the racing teams that belonged to a consortium known as F.I.S.A. – not to be confused with the sport's governing body FISA which came into existence later. F.I.S.A. was the Federation Italiana Scuderie Automobilsche, an amalgam of several Italian teams which joined together to promote and support Italian drivers in the higher echelons of the sport. F.I.S.A. was the official entrant of Baghetti's Ferrari 156 at the non-championship Siracusa Grand Prix, scheduled for 25 April, where it was thought the young and aspiring driver could do well in the face of a lacklustre opposition, an expectation which changed when virtually all the serious Grand Prix teams made the long journey across Europe to the race.

Baghetti told Graham Gauld that Enzo Ferrari had been impressed with his times at Monza in the short-wheelbase Ferrari and decided to draft him into the works sports car team for Sebring in March, as much to give him some experience with bigger engines as to acknowledge what he had managed to do with the GT car at Monza. Baghetti was teamed with Belgian Willy Mairesse for Sebring in a 250TR/61 which they handed over to von Trips and Ginther when von Trips suffered broken steering in the rear-engined six-cylinder 246SP. Hill and Olivier Gendebien went on to win in another 250TR/61 and von Trips, Ginther, Baghetti and Willy Mairesse shared second, while Pedro and Ricardo Rodriguez, who had led several times in their NART 250 TR/60, were third. Enzo Ferrari was impressed again.

However, there was no real hint that Baghetti was about to burst on to the international stage. In hindsight, it appears that this was a man on his way, but at the time this was never so clear. Phil Hill, Ginther and von Trips appeared to be the mainstays of the 1961 Ferrari Formula 1 year. The early season activity in motor racing served to mask what would develop as the year wore on, and the Baghetti 'phenomenon' was perhaps indicative of the surprises to come.

The British motor sport press, *Autosport* in particular, had shared the indignant response of the British teams that the new 1500cc rules were unworkable, that racing would be slower and probably more dangerous and the spectators wouldn't like it. As late as 10 March Managing Editor Gregor Grant remained very cautious about what 1961 would bring, still choosing to be suspicious of Ferrari's claims of 190bhp for the new 120-degree V6, predicting that 'this could well be a Lotus year', and that Cooper, Lotus and BRM were all ahead of Ferrari on road-holding. Grant even implied that the new Ferrari was taking suspension ideas from last year's Cooper-Climax, and if the brakes were good, it was because they were British-developed disc brakes! The following week Grant said it would be some time before the speeds of the 1500cc cars would match their predecessors. He lamented the lack of following the proposed alternative Inter-Continental Formula was getting, arguing also that drivers of the new cars would have to race more spectacularly to go fast and that would attract 'the sort of spectators who find their thrills in small circuit, stock car events'!

The arguments about the wisdom of the rule change and the early season success of the British teams without the presence of Ferrari continued and both issues seemed to cloud the experts' powers of prediction for 1961. Teams still held on to hopes that the Inter-Continental Formula would somehow be successful, and that a British engine would emerge which would be competitive with anything the Italians could develop. This optimism ran clearly in the face of all the testing and trial runs the rear-engined Ferraris were given in 1960. It wasn't that Ferrari had developed a new rear-engined car in secret, it was that the press and the other teams didn't want to believe it would work.

Giancarlo Baghetti, who came from relative obscurity to win his first three Formula 1 races. (Jim Gleave/Atlantic Art)

Autosport's technical wizard Tom Pritchard produced a very thoughtful analysis of the factors determining likely power output for the 1500cc engines. One of his conclusions was that, on the basis of past experience, form and comparison with the other manufacturers, Ferrari might just have what it would take to produce the power it was claiming. Pritchard's thoughts were perhaps pushed to one side when British cars and engines had good results in the very first races in the new formula, and Ferrari had a long-standing reputation for overstating its power outputs in new engines. To some extent this reputation aided Ferrari's plans for 1961, as a number of teams didn't believe it would produce what it claimed – doubts the sceptics would come to regret.

Unlike modern Formula 1, with no races other than those run as World Championship Grand Prix, the early '60s were almost overrun by the number of competitions taking place regularly. Stirling Moss had rung down the curtain on the 2.5-litre formula in Grand Prix with his victory at the United States event at Riverside, California, in November 1960, and this was followed by further wins in the non-World Championship races in South Africa run to 1500cc F2 rules. Moss's F2 Porsche was a potent force in South Africa, bringing him first in the Cape Grand Prix and then again at the East London Grand Prix. Jack Brabham followed Jo Bonnier home, so it was Porsche first and second and Cooper third to complete the 1960 season.

1961 got off to a very early start as all the serious stars were immediately in transit to New Zealand, where Jack Brabham and Bruce McLaren led another Cooper-Climax 1–2, this being the fourth year in a row that Cooper won at the New Zealand Grand Prix and the fourth year in a row that there was a new lap record at Ardmore. This 7 January race was in two heats to sort the grid positions for the Grand Prix final. Brabham scored another win a week later at Christchurch in near-flood conditions which prevailed for the Lady Wigram Trophy on 14 January. Moss followed Brabham in an accident-damaged Rob Walker Lotus ahead of Angus Hyslop's Cooper, Bruce McLaren and Denis Hulme. Clark, Bonnier, Surtees and Salvadori all suffered mechanical ailments in the dreadful conditions. The third New Zealand round at Dunedin on 28 January went to the Cooper-Climax which Denis Hulme had borrowed from the Yeoman Credit team. The only Ferrari presence in these races was the Dino chassis with Testa Rossa engine, used to very good effect by the hard-driving Pat Hoare in a car that is still used regularly in European historic races. With the international troop off to Australia, the final New Zealand Gold Star race, as the series was called, did in fact go to Hoare's front-engined Dino. Johnnie Mansel was there for the Waimate 50 in his TecMec Maserati, as was Bob Smith in the Ferrari Super Squalo. All three cars can be found together on historic race grids as this is being written!

Just as *Autosport* (10 February 1961) was announcing that Stirling Moss had taken the next 'down-under' race at Warwick Farm, Coventry-Climax's Chief Engineer W.T.F. Hassan took the unusual step of having a full statement about the company's engine plans published in the motor-sport journals:

As is well known the 2.5-litre Coventry-Climax type "FPF" engine which has been raced so successfully to the old Formula 1 of 2.5-litres was designed as a 1.5-litre engine, and the increased capacity was obtained only by the acceptance of a bore and stroke dictated purely by existing dimensions of crankcase, bearings, etc., and not from choice. The resulting stroke was too long and imposed an upper limit of 7,000rpm which seriously curtailed the potential power. The engines developed extremely good power at the permitted crankshaft speed, and although they won the races, they did not achieve 100bhp per litre which we now accept as a minimum target for a modern racing engine. The small dimension increase which is physically possible, leaves the capacity still well below three litres. It imposes considerably greater inertia loadings and because of this, the permissible crankshaft speed is reduced and also, therefore, the potential power. Should the speed restriction be ignored, then the reliability is very seriously impaired. It is, therefore, quite obvious that the existing 2.5-litre Coventry-Climax G.P. engine, whether modified or not, will not compete satisfactorily with full 3-litre engines. The fact of the matter is that whereas the Inter-Continental Formula was suggested in order to prolong the life of the existing 2.5-litre engines and cars, it has actually made the engines redundant, and thereby complicated the problems of constructors and engine builders to an even greater extent than did the change to Formula 1. Apart from the problems peculiar to the 2.5-litre engine there is another factor which is far more important and concerns the work in connection with Formula 1 – 1.5-litre engines. It is a fact that when the new formula was announced we were requested by the constructors, and other interested parties, to produce suitable engines. We agreed, and have since vigorously pursued the matter, having put in hand a number of considerably improved four-cylinder Mk.II engines for 1961, and an entirely new engine for 1962.

This 'entirely new engine' was, of course, the V8 which would take some time to arrive, much to the dismay of many teams, but Hassan told the author a few years ago, when discussing the rule change, that the early '60s was a time when teams expected Coventry-Climax 'to pull the wool over our own eyes just like some of the teams managed to do to themselves'. It was also a time when the industry was a bit more forthright about discussing its dilemmas. In spite of Coventry-Climax's doubts about the Inter-Continental formula, the CSI announced World Championship status for a 200-mile race at Brands Hatch in August, and the British Racing Sports Car Club also announced that Brands Hatch would be the venue for the Silver City International Trophy for Inter-Continental cars.

Meanwhile, the race at Warwick Farm in Sydney approached. During the three weeks since the previous round at Ardmore many of the overseas drivers had taken time to go shark fishing or holiday in Fiji, the weather had changed and Moss again was on top form; out of fourteen starters, he was one of only four drivers to survive the scorching

Australian heat, leading the other Lotus of Innes Ireland and the Coopers of Bib Stillwell and Austin Miller. Roy Salvadori took the final race for the 2.5-litre cars in the Gold Star series with a victory at Longford, Tasmania, a race enhanced by the sight of Jack Brabham, who had retired, standing by the side of the road waving a board to Salvadori and urging him on. Salvadori was struggling after an incident earlier in the race when a stone shattered his goggles and he drove with glass lodged in his eye.

In early March, the British motoring press published the first details of the Ferraris that had been launched in February, confirming the engines as being of two types: the 120-degree V6 of 1476cc and 190bhp, and the 65-degree V6 with 180bhp. By this time Gregor Grant was beginning to hedge his bets, hinting that the Ferraris would have a great power advantage at many circuits, but nevertheless casting suspicion on the team's ability to deliver what was promised and citing overstated power outputs from the past. Grant argued that Coventry-Climax was just as likely to produce 100bhp per litre as the Italians and would probably be more reliable; hence the British cars would be far more successful in 1961 than Ferrari. His patriotic wishful thinking had no bounds.

On the driver front, the coming season was beginning to take shape, though the full line-up would not emerge until at least the Monaco Grand Prix. Phil Hill and Wolfgang von Trips were the only definite names attached to Ferrari at this point. BRM had been truly caught out, hoping

The 65-degree engine block on the right, with the 2.4-litre 246, the medium block on the left. (John Godfrey Collection)

The opposite end of the 65-degree block. (John Godfrey Collection)

Side view of the 65-degree engine. (John Godfrey Collection)

that the 2.5-litre formula would be reprieved, and was going to depend on Coventry-Climax for a 1.5-litre engine, and on drivers Graham Hill and Tony Brooks. The latter was a man who would come to regret his decision to soldier on with BRM. Innes Ireland and Jim Clark shared top billing at Lotus, while two-times World Champion Jack Brabham was going for a third title with Cooper; New Zealander Bruce McLaren was in the Cooper team as well. Early rumours that Stirling Moss would drive for Porsche were put to rest with the announcement that he would again be with Rob Walker's private team – both a Lotus and Cooper being used for 1961. Up to this point, Moss had been the only driver to win a Grand Prix in a Lotus, and there was strong pressure for him to join a works team to gain a real chance of the World Championship, but instead he chose the option of two types of car at Rob Walker's to give him a winning edge. Equipe National Belge planned to run the Emeryson effort, with a car for two Belgians – Olivier Gendebien and that extraordinarily aggressive driver, Willy Mairesse. As the Emeryson, with the heavy Maserati engine, was to register only non-qualifications for Gendebien and Lucien Bianchi at Monaco and another for yet a further Belgian, Andre Pilette, at Monza, this would provide positive opportunities for Gendebien and Mairesse, though they didn't know it at the time. The UDT-Laystall team started the year with older Lotus 18s for Henry Taylor and then picked up Lucien Bianchi. Yeoman Credit Racing had Cooper T-53s for Salvadori and the promising John Surtees, as opposed to the works team's T-55. Rumours also persisted about the imminent appearance of a rear-engined Maserati, and the OSCA F1 car.

With the announcement of the entries for the first serious Formula 1 race of 1961 – the non-championship Grand Prix of Brussels to be run over three 100-kilometre heats of the Heysel street circuit on the edge of the Belgian capital – Gurney and Bonnier were confirmed for Porsche, and only von Trips was entered by Ferrari. In the meantime, the inhospitable Snetterton circuit in Norfolk hosted Britain's first international event of the new season, with a combined grid for the Inter-Continental and the 1.5-litre cars, now being dubbed the 'F1' cars. Reports of the meeting still cast doubt on the competitiveness of the smaller engined machines, seemingly ignoring the fact that Surtees and Salvadori were on the front row in Coopers and Henry Taylor was on the second row. Brabham won overall, as well as taking the Inter-Continental class some 6mph quicker than Surtees in the F1 section. Perhaps it was round one to the sceptics!

Following the international trek for all the stars to the wide open airfield circuit at Sebring in late March, not one but two Formula 1 races took place on Easter Monday: one at Goodwood, Sussex, and the other at Pau in France. In retrospect, it is difficult to conceive how the inaugural races for the new 1.5-litre formula should take place on the same day. Nevertheless, at Goodwood, crowds of nearly 50,000 braved unpleasant spring conditions as the International '100' for the new 1.5-litre cars shared the bill with an Inter-Continental round for the Lavant Cup. John Surtees set the pace for the new category by turning a quickest lap of 1 minute 28 seconds, or 98.18mph as his finely prepared Yeoman Credit

Cooper-Climax hurtled into the lead with Stirling Moss on his tail. Moss remained there for thirty-two of the forty-one laps when a bent valve dropped him to fourth behind Surtees, Graham Hill (BRM) and Roy Salvadori (Cooper). Salvadori had driven one of his finest races before he recovered from a spin, while Tony Brooks went off on lap 27 and was alleged to have forgotten that he had an on-board starter. Every car in the race was powered by a Coventry-Climax engine, and Surtees' fastest lap was 3mph quicker than McLaren's fastest in the Inter-Continental race held earlier in the day, which was won by Moss. Press reports still persisted in arguing that the 1.5-litre cars 'looked slower even if they weren't'. The reality of the new machines' potential was only slowly dawning, and the Ferraris hadn't appeared yet. Round two had definitely been won by the newcomers.

In the French Pyrenees, another huge Easter crowd turned up for the first significant race on the continent for the new season, the Pau Grand Prix. While Moss, Surtees, Allison, Salvadori, McLaren, Brooks, Ireland, Halford and Henry Taylor were all getting soaked in Britain, Jim Clark, Jo Bonnier, Jack Brabham, Trevor Taylor, Maurice Trintignant and Lorenzo Bandini were enjoying brilliant sunshine in the little spa resort surrounded by wonderful mountain scenery.

Jim Clark took his Lotus 18-Climax off into an early lead, and when Brabham stopped with a faulty fuel pump, Clark was clear, though his engine wasn't particularly clean at high revs and he nearly ran out of fuel at the end. Bonnier brought another Lotus into second, ahead of the Maserati-engined Coopers of Bandini and Mario Cabral. Both Trevor Taylor and Clark reported later that the Lotus's handling over the twisty street circuit was excellent – a sign of things to come. Cabral, a talented Portuguese driver who never quite produced the results he might have been capable of, told the author some years later while they were both taking part in the Angolan sports car series, that he was surprised the Cooper-Maserati stayed on the road: 'If you put your foot down, sometimes the power was there and sometimes it wasn't, and the handling was unpredictable on this tight circuit. But I think Bandini drove it better than I did.' Cabral was to go a step further in 1964 when he ran the re-worked ATS, known as the Derrington-Francis, in its only Grand Prix at Monza. This car has also reappeared recently in historic events.

The following weekend the racing circus headed to Brussels and evidence was provided that the new 1500cc cars were not going to remain in the shadow of their bigger predecessors: John Surtees broke the old 2.5-litre record in the second of the three heats. Even *Autosport* had to admit that it had been wrong and the new formula looked as if it was going to be quick. Most of the teams hadn't even brought their new cars. Ferrari remained quiet and didn't show up for the Brussels Grand Prix because final development work and testing was being done on the 156. A cautious decision to debut the new car at Siracusa in Sicily was made by Chiti.

In Brussels, Jo Bonnier made the Porsche threat look serious by planting his car on pole for the first heat, with McLaren in the centre of the three-by-two grid and Gurney's Porsche on the outside. Bonnier was on good form and the Porsche was producing enough power for him to dominate the heat and set a new lap record, while Roy Salvadori continued to demonstrate his skill by taking second spot when several of the top runners were penalised for a jumped start. Surtees flew through from sixth in heat two in his Yeoman Credit Cooper to challenge Bonnier but ran into the back of him, taking them both out and leaving the door open for Brabham and McLaren. Innes Ireland made a spectacular start in his Lotus to lead the third heat ahead of Brabham, privateer Tony Marsh, McLaren and Moss. Ireland, already establishing his reputation as a brave but often wild driver, just survived flying through telephone poles and traffic lights when he came off the street circuit, allowing Brabham into the lead to start a long and exciting battle with Moss. Brabham stayed in front and Moss was $\frac{1}{10}$ second behind at the finish, with McLaren third. Because the results were aggregated, Brabham won from McLaren and there were few people who went away thinking the 1.5-litre cars were going to be boring. In this race-packed pre-Championship season Stirling Moss even managed to go off and win the Prix de Vienna at the Austrian Aspern circuit in the Rob Walker Lotus, having to fight off Tim Parnell in one of his best F1 races.

Less than a week before the Siracusa Grand Prix, Ferrari's entries for the race were still clouded in mystery: Phil Hill was thought to be entered in the 120-degree V6 with further cars for von Trips and Ginther. The racing world had little knowledge of what was going on in the Italian team and had no idea that Chiti was still far from ready to show his hand. Only three days before the Sicilian race, however, all the British teams turned up for the non-Championship Aintree '200', another soaking wet event organised by the British Automobile Racing Club, and there were still seven races on the schedule before the first Championship round at Monaco. Brabham led McLaren home at Aintree in a race that was notable for the fine drive through the field by Masten Gregory in a Cooper, and for the lacklustre performance of the BRM. Tony Brooks was about to start a season that was to take the fire and enthusiasm out of him – sad for someone apparently destined to take the world championship not long before.

Only days after Aintree, the Siracusa Grand Prix was scheduled for a Tuesday, 25 April, a day which would jolt the Grand Prix world into the realisation that the 1.5-litre cars had arrived and that Ferrari had been busy doing their homework for the past twelve months. Virtually no one had seen the new car with its stunningly shaped bodywork and sculptured front end. The 'sharknose' was here to take the racing world by surprise.

After Monza and the Italian Grand Prix the previous September, where von Trips took the F2 class in the rear-engined prototype chassis 0008, the car was sent to contest the Modena Grand Prix on 2 October. Chiti then made the decision to convert the chassis to the new 1961 specifications. Immediately after Modena it was back to the factory to begin the task of getting ready for the new season and the new regulations. This included, fairly late in the year after confidence in the chassis and engine had been established, designing and building a new body. The prototype had been quick but somewhat heavy and ungainly-looking and a number of ideas had been considered before Chiti revealed the 'new look'. This included the dramatic treatment of the front end and nose which would eventually come to characterise the whole car, the 'sharknose'.

The 156 'sharknose' was not the first nor the only car to use this approach to front-end design. Chiti, according to journalist and self-styled automotive consultant trouble-shooter Hans Tanner, appropriated the idea from Medardo Fantuzzi, who had used a twin-nostril approach during his Maserati days, especially while working on the 'piccolo' 250F. It was Hans Tanner himself who claimed credit for introducing the idea to Fantuzzi while consulting for Maserati. He in turn gives credit for the idea to the little-known Sacha-Gordine project inspired by a French film producer who aimed to bring France back to Grand Prix glory in the early 1950s. His design featured a radical dohc V8 and an ultra low shape that was years ahead of its time. It incorporated well-thought-out twin-nostril air intakes to feed two front radiators. Sadly, though, the cars were only part built, and the project disappeared as quickly as it had come about. A number of racing car manufacturers copied the design after it appeared at Ferrari, the Wainer Formula Junior being a tidy if somewhat scaled-down version.

Chiti, having more or less convinced Enzo Ferrari by late 1960 that the rear- or mid-engine machine was the direction Grand Prix cars and eventually sports cars should go, managed then to get the new body shape, and particularly the nose, wind-tunnel tested. This underlined its characteristic of giving better penetration than the conventional nose scoop in use at the time. Chiti recalled to Piero Casucci (1987) that the technical office at Ferrari would draw up new plans at an enormous rate, and that it was probably the model-maker Casoli who produced the first scale model of the twin-nostril front end for testing in the company's small but effective tunnel. This work was going on at a time when considerable research was under way into aerodynamics for the new range of sports racing cars, and it is no accident that the same type of nose appeared on the 246 SP and other SP cars for 1961 and 1962. Which came first is a matter for conjecture, and the author has never found convincing evidence to pinpoint either the clear Ferrari origins of the sharknose, or even the first use of the term 'sharknose' to describe it.

While the outward appearance of the new Ferrari that made its public debut at Siracusa was nothing short of stunning, the work beneath the skin had been going on at a frantic pace. Chiti had been developing an improved version of the 65-degree car since the previous September, and had focused almost entirely on the new 120-degree layout over the entire 1960/1 winter period. The intention had been to debut two cars, the new 120-degree machine and chassis 0008 in its revised form for 1961, but with the 65-degree engine which had been thoroughly tested by now over a considerable period.

Chiti's near obsession with the 120-degree engine and his endless changes meant the car would still not race. He had intended that the

120-degree engine would be the mainstay of 1961 and would replace the 65-degree unit at the beginning of the season. Ferrari planning, however, was rarely as accurate as intended, and the original engines carried on not only through 1961 but almost until the end of the 'sharknose' period, if not to the end of the 156 reign. The 65-degree engine disappeared altogether only after the 1962 German Grand Prix.

For 1961, Chiti was anxious to exploit what he began to perceive as Ferrari's advantage over the opposition by early acceptance of the new regulations. While Ferrari had announced a 3-litre engine for the Inter-Continental Formula, it never appeared in any of these races, and all the development went into the 1.5-litre car. The move to the rear-engined format had allowed greater opportunity to exploit the use of a lower and wider configuration than had ever been possible with the front-engined cars. Chiti was after higher revs than the 65-degree unit could manage while still wanting to maintain the same level of reliability. The use of the wider V between the two engine banks provided better internal balance, and also allowed it to sit lower in the chassis, so that the lines of the body could be substantially lower as well. The wider V also allowed flexibility for employing either carburettors or fuel injection, a development Chiti was enthusiastic to try out though it wasn't followed up seriously until 1963.

Three-quarter view of the 1.5-litre Dino engine. (John Godfrey Collection)

The immediate origins of the 156's engine were, of course, in the Dino 246, and though the first use in rear-engine form in 1960 looked revolutionary for Ferrari, this was still a 2.5-litre unit modified to 1.5-litres. It was reasonably compact for the time but still heavy. The 120-degree approach would permit further lightening and, more importantly, more effective placement in the chassis. The 120-degree engine would never have fitted in the front-engined 246 but it was perfect for providing Chiti with the chance to do what he really wanted – to integrate engine and chassis development in a way that Enzo Ferrari himself never actively encouraged. Ferrari's long-held view that the heart of any racing car was its engine, a view that arguably delayed for years the design of a modern chassis, form part of the Ferrari legend. Writers like Mike Lawrence and Brock Yates go a step further in arguing that Ferrari rarely brought about innovation himself, and though he took himself seriously as an engineer, his engineering contribution was less important than his use of people such as Chiti and Colombo, who were much closer to being engineering and design geniuses.

It was Chiti's intention that the 120-degree unit should power the 156, but the short stroke 65-degree engine which had evolved from the 246 into the F2 car power-plant was now fitted to the first cars for 1961, a fact that led many people to assume that Ferrari had intended to use two engine types. At the time, however, there was little to distinguish the two engines externally; the only apparent difference to the spectator was that the 65-degree engine had a single fine-mesh covering over the carburettors and the 120-degree unit had a double-mesh cover. The 'prototype' chassis 0008 which ran in 1960 had a large plexi-glass cover, and at least one 1961 prototype had exposed and raised intakes for the carburettors. Alan Henry (1989) describes the differences in the chassis for each type of engine, the 120-degree unit being 'installed in a tubular chassis dominated by main upper and lower longerons of 1½in diameter. Those chassis designated to accept the 120-degree engine had the upper longeron bowed out slightly in order to facilitate installation of the wider engine, while the frames intended for the narrower 65-degree unit had the upper tubes running parallel to the lower.' It remains unclear whether this was a simple modification which Chiti undertook when he had the 120-degree engine near completion, or whether he started out with the idea of two, at least slightly, different chassis.

It is probably true to say that part of Chiti's genius was his ability to study the work of the masters and improve on it. In this case the masters were Lampredi and Jano. Lampredi had done design work on a 120-degree engine in the early 1950s which had never reached fruition, but a number of key principles of this type of layout had already been clarified. Chiti took the principles and set out to improve upon them, with major effort devoted to making the whole unit lighter. This involved the use of shorter connecting rods and smaller diameter big ends, and effecting a more straightforward and simpler crankshaft with the wider-angle layout, in conjunction with the usual rods forged from blanks retaining double bolt big ends. Chiti initiated the use of a disposable oil filter, a first for Ferrari, which was placed at the front of the engine. The front of the crankshaft drove the scavenge and oil pressure pumps, though the earlier Dino practice was followed in having the oil gallery down the centre of the V.

Chiti took a leaf out of Jano's book and improved upon it in the way the engine banks were laid out. To quote Hans Tanner's detailed account (1984, p. 139):

One major difference between earlier Dinos and the Chiti-designed 120-degree engine was that the cylinder bank offset was transposed. Jano in the first Dino followed the Lancia system of off-setting the left hand bank ahead of the right hand bank. Chiti reversed this and moved the right hand bank ahead of the left hand. This changeover was apparently not for any specific technical reason and was probably more to bring the 120-degree design in line with all previous Ferrari V12 models. Internally the Chiti engine differed from the older Dinos in that experience with the earlier engine had been well heeded and resulted in a certain amount of simplification in the new power plant. Each cylinder head was held down by eight studs instead of the original twelve. Chain drive to the camshafts was retained, but between the cam sprockets, the chain was made to run straight across as on the V8 Lancia, instead of being drawn down around an additional idler sprocket.

Each bank had its own double-roller chain system driven from the two half-speed gears on the nose of the crankshaft. The twin distributors splayed out at 120 degrees in front of the block were also driven by these gears through spiral pinions.

Chiti retained the Jano principle of using wide cam lobes acting on the mushroom tappets in a cylinder head Chiti had simplified but which was still very similar to earlier Dino design. Chiti altered the usual practice in the earlier engine where both cam housings had been machined in the same plane, and instead employed the practice of cutting at right angles to the valve stems. This resulted in a valve angle of 28 degrees from the vertical for the intakes and a slightly larger 32 degrees for the exhausts, with a total angle of 60 degrees, the same as in the original Dino. The author is again indebted to the research work of Hans Tanner for explaining the detailed developments Chiti undertook and tracing his elaborate efforts in utilising two intake valve diameters to produce differing power curves. Chiti's knowledge of and experimentation with gas velocities allowed him to produce an engine with considerable flexibility, using a smaller valve format to provide impressive torque figures, and a larger valve format to increase top end power substantially.

Tanner (1984, p. 140) recognised Chiti's ability to develop a particular engine principle and achieve varying results from experimenting with it:

Both these valve sizes [the two different intake valve diameter sizes on the 120-degree engine] were designed for the 65-degree and the 120-degree engine layouts, and initial power outputs for both types of engine were calculated at 160 to 170bhp for the smaller valve and 180 to 190 bhp for the larger valve. These outputs were increased through development in the 1961 to 1963 period, during which time Chiti (before leaving to found ATS in 1962) experimented with, first, twin-plug heads, then three-plug still with two valves, followed by two plugs with three valves, and finally returned to one plug with four valves. Little success was achieved, but in 1962 the initial two-valve twin-plug development heads were fitted and raced. Because of the better balance of the 120-degree engine it produced slightly more power due to the raising of the safe rev limit from 9,500rpm to 10,000rpm, an increase from 4080 to 4300ft per minute of corrected piston speed.

As 1961 progressed, both the 65- and 120-degree engines were showing very reasonable power figures on the test bench, and the weight savings achieved had not been at the cost of either power or reliability, at least as far as early testing was able to demonstrate. The five-speed transaxle which had appeared on the 1960 prototype had now been transferred to the new car, including the multiple-plate clutch exposed at the rear of the gearbox, and this was driven by a lengthy shaft from the engine which passed below the gearbox. This differed from transmissions developed by a number of other teams who included the clutch as part of the engine unit. The exposed arrangement was presumably to aid cooling of the Ferrari clutch, a known weakness from previous seasons. As we will see, gearbox modifications would become something of an issue in the car's reliability and performance, much to the dismay particularly of Phil Hill who would be on the receiving end of the gearbox woes. Not that Hill disliked Ferrari gearboxes – in fact he had gone out of his way at times to praise them, especially the F1 boxes. He writes in Grayson (1975, p. 224) that the new 156 'felt so good. It had a five-speed gearbox, non-synchronized, that was astoundingly easy to shift. Nothing to it. Ferrari could make beautiful gearboxes, contrary to later reputation. The only difficult Ferrari gearboxes were the synchronized ones used in the later Gran Turismo cars. These were heavy to shift, had too much travel and balked when you tried to hurry, but there was never a problem with the Formula cars.' The way in which gearboxes would be developed, however, and the timing of fitting a new box into a car, would cause Hill some hard moments.

Because Chiti's plan was to get the engine as close to the middle of the chassis as possible in order to achieve a low centre of gravity, it was sensible to employ the casing for the transaxle between the engine and the final drive, effectively making it a spacer, and, according to both Tanner and Henry, this would have allowed Ferrari to drop the Inter-Continental 2.9 unit in if the alternative Championship gained momentum. It is, however, difficult to determine whether that possibility was a greater influence on the layout than another factor: this arrange-ment permitted easier ratio changes, and the rearward clutch also allowed for the fitting of the ring gear and starter. Tanner (1989, p. 140) describes the complexity of the transmission:

The gear train up to the clutch from the engine shaft was readily inter-changeable. To change the overall gear ratios, the entire clutch and back cover plate complete with its built-in hydraulic clutch withdrawal caliper was taken off. The two gears were laid out so that the ratio provided would never be higher than one to one and most often would be a reduction between unity and one to one, so that the clutch and attached input shaft to the gearbox would usually run at less than engine speed. The primary or input shaft of the all-indirect gearbox was placed on the right and slightly below the centre line of the secondary or output shaft, which directly drove the spiral bevel final drive gears. The box housed five constant-mesh forward speeds on the earlier cars and six on some of the later experimental models, all without synchromesh, and was equipped with its own pressure lubrication system.

The 156 suspension departed somewhat from what had been tried on the 1960 prototype, and tubular wishbones of unequal length with coil springs and damper units mounted outboard replaced the earlier arrangement of tubular rear wishbones and forged ones at the front. The mounting angles of the new layout were also all different, given the changes to the chassis and engine placement. The existing vertical suspension post was revamped to accommodate the rear-facing steering arm and in the process gained considerable stiffness. New adjustable-length rear wishbones were added. While this aided the cause of experimentation, the wishbones were always thought to be rather long and the suspension not quite as refined as the work of some other teams. Ferrari's practice of using quite long rear wishbones continued for a considerable period, and the author was very recently able to examine their use on the 512S (chassis 1006).

Ferrari was one of the last, if not the last, team to use centre-locking wire wheels on 15in Borrani rims. The Dunlop disc brakes which had been found on the Grand Prix cars of recent years were retained with conventional front outboard layout, but with a change to the rear, which were now mounted inboard. Twin universal joints were fitted to the half-shafts with sliding ball splines at the inner ends. The hubs at the rear were now carried in the suspension posts that had been altered.

The drivers of the new cars would find their feet accommodated by the placement of the rack-and-pinion steering and 12 volt battery/booster combination. Further forward was the three-section radiator with one section on either side carrying water and the centre section carrying oil to and from the oil tank located behind the radiator, all tucked neatly behind the twin intakes of the shapely 'sharknose'.

Both the F1 cars and the new sports cars appeared at the annual Ferrari press conference in February, and Doug Nye (1979) was of the opinion that the 'sharknose' front end might have appeared first on one of the sports cars, probably the 246 Dino. While there had clearly been testing of the new 156 in various forms through 1960, and in the updated version in late 1960, it is virtually impossible to tell exactly when the 'sharknose'-style body ran for the first time. The cars had been run before the press day in February, and Ginther was pictured testing the unpainted prototype with the 120-degree engine, presumably also in

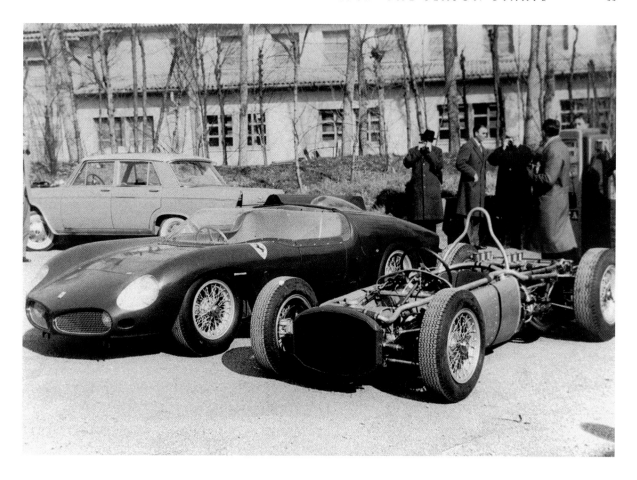

February. This was at Modena with the new chassis 0001. Tests with this car continued in March, and Ginther seems likely to have been driving it at Monza on 14 March, the day when von Trips rolled the 246SP, and Ginther and Chiti got together to try some aircraft-inspired trim tabs and a rear vertical fence – the first rear spoiler – and thereby changed the course of racing aerodynamics. Ginther then declared this the best sports car he had ever driven.

Phil Hill remembered testing the rear-engined car properly for the first time at Zandvoort in 1960, and when interviewed in California in August 2000 recalled:

The 156 makes its debut at the February 1961 Ferrari press day, with 120-degree engine but without the 'sharknose' body. Alongside is the new 246SP sports car. (Raymond Jenkins)

> I was tremendously impressed to see how deceived we had been by merely our placement in the car, by being that close to the unstable end of the car which made such a huge difference at a place like Zandvoort. Of course, Zandvoort was the very place that you didn't want to be at the back. My first impressions of the chassis were that it was very good. I don't know why we stuck with so much negative camber . . . that's baffling. They couldn't come up with an arrangement that didn't have so much negative camber in it. I can't remember when I first saw it with the 'sharknose'. I don't know if that was at the factory or at Monte Carlo, but I didn't test it before Monte Carlo in that form.

It was during testing in the period between Sebring and the numerous other single-seater races going on in April 1961 that Ginther began to have oil scavenging problems. He was driving the 120-degree car at Modena, and though a formal works entry had been made for him for the Siracusa race on 25 April, this was withdrawn and another made in the name of F.I.S.A. for Giancarlo Baghetti in the 65-degree car, chassis 0008. This was the prototype from the previous year which had been seriously modified to become the first racing version of the new 'sharknose'. Von Trips had won the race in 1960 in the front-engined F2 Dino at an average speed of 162.161kph, and this average was fully expected to be beaten soon after the first practice session.

Sicilian confusion threatened to reign as the local posters advertising the race variously gave the start time as 2.30, 3.00, and 3.30pm. Entry numbers were unexpectedly high, as most of the teams had decided to use Siracusa as a serious test session prior to the start of the World Championship season. Cars had to be transported out to Sicily by air as the race came only days after the Aintree meeting. The date, 25 April, a Tuesday, had been chosen because it was a Sicilian holiday to celebrate the Allied landings during the Second World War.

Team Manager Tavoni and three factory race mechanics were there to look after Baghetti, and Piero Taruffi was also on hand to 'coach' him. F.I.S.A. had Baghetti, Lorenzo Bandini and Renato Pirocchi in their line-up, but Baghetti was the favourite based on his recent sports car test times and the support he got from Dragoni. Works Porsches, which had looked threatening in testing and early season races, were provided for Dan Gurney and Jo Bonnier. While the British teams had begun to worry about what Ferrari might produce, they soon found that the Porsches were to give them a real scare too. The Porsche Typ 718 was originally a development of the RSK sports car and more recently had drawn inspiration from the F2 car, before now appearing at the front of an F1 grid. It looked as much a threat as the Ferrari to all the British teams, who now realised they had been caught on the hop by not getting to grips with the new regulations.

A number of the British entrants had been forced to miss the Sunday practice because of the problems encountered by the freight airlines in getting the cars from Liverpool to Catania in a very short space of time. As Sunday's practice got under way without the cars that were still in transit from Aintree, the expectations were that Gurney and Bonnier would dominate the fairly mundane group already present. A somewhat cautious Baghetti went out for his first taste of F1 – there is little or no evidence that he had any time in the car for serious testing beforehand. (Later in the season, Ricardo Rodriguez would have the same experience of sitting in an F1 car for the first time on a Wednesday and qualifying on a Saturday.) It wasn't long before Baghetti had thrust the Ferrari round the track in under 2 minutes – the only car to do so, though there were few who realistically believed he would be at the front of the grid after Moss, Clark and co. arrived for the next day's session. Nevertheless, he was still the quickest at 1 minute 58.8 seconds which equalled the previous 1.5-litre record for the fast circuit. Gurney and Bonnier couldn't break 2 minutes, and the rest of the field consisted of an odd assortment of Emerysons and Cooper-Maseratis.

A strong wind was blowing as all the cars were ready for the Monday practice, with Bonnier the first to beat Baghetti's Sunday time. Panic began to set in as the end of the session approached, and everyone was desperate for a decent time. Hill and Brabham got into the 58 second bracket, then Baghetti went out and completed two quite slow laps that had the opposition puzzled, after which he calmly put his foot down and set a 1 minute 57.8 seconds record. John Surtees posted the same time in the Yeoman Credit Cooper-Climax, which featured a body that the team had designed themselves and was an improvement on the works cars. It had a smaller radiator opening, a slimmer nose and raked windscreen, a narrower body and a tidier and more compact rear body section.

Then Baghetti, who had been quietly sitting in the car, with no customary Ferrari chaos going on around him, no suspension setting changes taking place, no tyre changes, lapped in 1 minute 57 seconds without appearing to try. In the last lap before the rain came in torrents, Gurney was out on the Porsche's limit and shaved a tenth of a second off Baghetti's time for pole.

Motorsport's Denis Jenkinson was on hand to cover this important race and was almost rapturous about the Ferrari's sound and Baghetti's ability to go down through the gears without a change of note from the exhausts. Jenks took the trouble to provide a full report on the Ferrari developments:

This was the first racing appearance of the 1961 Ferrari and though it followed the lines of the F2 car used last year it was an entirely new car. The front wishbones were forged while the rear ones were welded tube construction and the chassis frame was of large diameter tubing like a Cooper rather than small diameter like a Lotus. The layout was a space frame with the engine behind the driver, coupled to a 5-speed and reverse gear-box, on the end of which was mounted the flywheel and clutch, exposed to the air. At the extreme end of the mechanism was mounted the hydraulically-operated plunger which depressed the toggles of the clutch assembly, the drive from the engine passing right through the gearbox/differential housing to the clutch and back into the gearbox. The toothed flywheel and clutch body were in one unit and the starter motor was on a cradle on top of the gearbox and engaging with the toothed flywheel; the 12-volt battery was carried at the front of the chassis, behind the oil tank, the two of them being mounted behind the radiator and above the rack and pinion steering mechanism. The short steering column passed through a chassis cross member and was carried in a bearing mounted behind the instrument panel, and fuel tanks formed the cockpit sides, the seat being well padded, and there also being blue upholstered pads along each upper chassis tube just below the driver's shoulders. A 10,000rpm indicator faced the driver, the gear gate was on the right and a curved Perspex screen extended along both sides of the body. The nose cowling was very low and flat and extended forward into a pointed snout with two "nostrils" to take air into the radiator, while the rear of the body finished in a blunt end with horizontal slats. A Perspex teardrop covered the three double-choke downdraught Weber carburettors, a small opening on the front on each side allowing air into the engine. At the rear of this Perspex cover and on each side were Perspex scoops directing air down into the bowels of the rear end to cool the inboard mounted disc brakes. The front discs were hub-mounted with the calipers mounted at the front, and naturally Borrani wire wheels were used. The two exhaust manifolds ended in long tail pipes stuck way out behind the car and for the first part of practice they had Italian "Snap" exhaust boosters on the ends, but these soon gave way to normal Ferrari shallow megaphones. (*Motorsport*, June, 1961, p. 474.)

It would appear that Jenks made the first reference to a 'nostril-nose', the term for the car which caught on among many British fans for a time. It was also Jenks who observed that the 'Ferrari certainly looked like a racing car, and it sounded like one. It went like one as well' – a practically hysterical comment for Jenks! It should also be noted that Doug Nye (Nye, 1979, p. 123) counters Jenks's view that this was a brand new car, identifying it as 'presumably the 1960 Monza tests prototype, since its chassis number was "0008" – apparently carrying on the 1960 Dino 156/246 serials'. Nye adds that as this was an Italian race there was no particular need to indulge in the usual practice of juggling chassis numbers for the carnets presented at the borders, and he thus assumes the chassis number on the car was 'genuine'; the author agrees with this.

In retrospect, it is interesting that Baghetti's performance in the car which was to go on to win Ferrari's first constructor's championship doesn't merit a significant account in the bulk of the books written about Ferrari, other than in Nye's work on the Dinos. Even Tanner overlooks the Siracusa race entirely. None of this mattered to Baghetti himself when the flag fell for the start of the 56-lap race, a total of 308 kilometres. A full 11 seconds covered the 19-car grid with Gurney, Baghetti and Surtees at the front and Pirocchi, Boffa, Mairesse and Wolfgang Seidel at the back. It was no surprise to the experts that the Ferrari came around at the end of the first lap down in seventh spot behind Surtees, Gurney, Bonnier, Ireland (Lotus), Brabham (Cooper), and Graham Hill (BRM) with Stirling Moss's Rob Walker Lotus-Climax on his tail.

Moss, who went on to play a crucial part in the 'sharknose' story as a competitor and then nearly a driver, spoke with the author about Siracusa:

It was a circuit I really liked because it was quick and was a proper road circuit. It wasn't a good race for us because we had just come from Aintree and the same engine had done the Aspern race, I think, so it had some problems and it wasn't very quick. I think I was only on the third row. At the time I didn't pay a lot of attention to Baghetti but in the race and afterwards we all knew the Ferrari was quick. You are never certain in some of these early season races about whether a car will be that good all year but the new Ferrari certainly looked good in

Phil Hill at Monaco in the Ferrari 156 Sharknose, 1961.
(Archive von Trips/Fodisch)

Phil Hill. (Graeme Simpson/Motor Racing Tradition)

Above: Carlo Chiti (in the dark suit) supervises a test session on 14 March 1961 of two of the 65-degree engined cars. (Archive von Trips/Fodisch) *Below*: Richie Ginther, left, and von Trips use Carlo Chiti's Fiat saloon as their vantage point from which to consider the 'sharknose' bodywork for the first time in its finished form at the Modena test track. (Archive von Trips/Fodisch)

Giancarlo Baghetti at Siracusa in Sicily, winning his first F1 race in the first event for the 156 'sharknose' in 1961. (John Blunsden/ *Motor Racing*)

Bonnier and Hill chase Ginther in second as the cars rush down from the Station hairpin to the right-hander before the tunnel, Monaco, 1961, (John Blunsden/*Motor Racing*)

Bonnier and Gurney in the Porsches lead Ginther and Hill out of the Station hairpin, Monaco, 1961. (John Blunsden/*Motor Racing*)

Richie Ginther in practice leads one
of the Coopers into the Hunzerug
at Zandvoort, 1961. (John
Blunsden/*Motor Racing*)

Ginther in the Hunzerug in practice
for the Dutch Grand Prix. (John
Blunsden/*Motor Racing*)

Ginther's chassis 0001 awaiting practice at Spa, 1961. Note the twin covers on the carburettors for the 120-degree engine. (Graham White)

Above: Luigi Bazzi warms up Gendebien's car, chassis 0002 painted yellow and with the 65-degree engine at Spa, 1961. (Graham White)
Below: Ginther's car ready for practice at Spa, 1961, with the carb covers removed to improve top speed. (Brian Joscelyne)

Wolfgang von Trips shortly before the start of the Italian Grand Prix, 1961. (John Blunsden/*Motor Racing*)

The line-up of cars at the Ferrari press day in February 1962. (John Godfrey Collection)

the race. I was behind him near the start but the engine was mis-firing and I dropped back. In the end I pushed it over the line just to finish [eighth] but it wasn't a good race.

While Gurney held the lead for the first lap, Baghetti was already using the Ferrari's power to get past Graham Hill and Jack Brabham – exalted company for the 'new boy' – and as Surtees had a short spell in front, Giancarlo then slipped past the works Lotus of Innes Ireland. The following lap saw the slipstreaming consequences as Gurney pulled out and went to the front again, and this time Baghetti was closing on the Porsche of Jo Bonnier. The familiar Italian roar that accompanies a racing Ferrari's move into the lead was audible all around the 5.5-kilometre circuit on lap 6 when Baghetti had not only pulled away from a surprised Bonnier but in virtually a single move had taken both Surtees and Gurney's leading Porsche. He then proceeded to pull out something

Baghetti in chassis 0008 at Siracusa in 1961. (BRSCC Archive)

of a margin. Giancarlo Baghetti, in his first ever F1 race, was leading the Siracusa Grand Prix.

Baghetti, seemingly unruffled and driving in a very relaxed manner, kept ahead of Gurney who was working hard to stay in contention, while Bonnier slipped back but held third. Surtees retired on the tenth lap with fuel pressure problems, and a fierce battle for fourth raged between Brabham, Hill and Ireland. Both Hill and Ireland would eventually retire, though there were several other contests down the field, one of them involving Stirling Moss, whose out-of-sorts Lotus was struggling with Willy Mairesse in the Belgian-entered Emeryson-Maserati. It was as Baghetti and Gurney came up to lap these two that Baghetti nearly threw it all away. Gurney slipped past into the lead, but Baghetti remained relaxed, and within a few laps had re-passed the silver Porsche and started to pull away as they came up to lap the eighth-placed Roy Salvadori in the second Yeoman Credit Cooper.

Salvadori, a driver who remains under-rated in spite of a long, successful career and some superb F1 performances, winced as he recounted the Siracusa race from the comfort of his spacious apartment overlooking Monaco harbour:

I didn't really like Siracusa very much. I thought the road was terrible, bumpy, you know, and off-camber and there were several places where it was very narrow. I was having a good race with Trintignant but you were very close to the edge of the road! I finished fifth which wasn't bad. It was a race where all the attention was on Gurney and Baghetti, as Baghetti was really driving a works car.

Roy Salvadori is one of those people who is not so nostalgic for the 'old days': 'There were a lot of slow cars going around at the back just making up the numbers. I like today's Grand Prix racing. There are fewer cars but they are much closer and the technology is more interesting.'

Baghetti then held on to a 5 second lead over Gurney for the final laps, lapping Bonnier in the process. Somewhat ungraciously, Bonnier refused to let Gurney lap him, though clearly the American was not going to catch Baghetti, who apparently made his only big mistake at the end of the race when he went down the escape road after the finish line. He stood in the pit lane afterwards and seemed to find it difficult to take in the enormity of what he had accomplished – winning his first Formula 1 race and beating all the top drivers of the day. He didn't have long to think about it as the hordes of Sicilian fans overwhelmed the pit lane to celebrate the achievement. The rest of the teams were left to consider what might happen when the 'regular' drivers got into the car.

Dan Gurney, who had had a good chance to change history by taking the race from Baghetti, told the author the impact the Ferrari had on him at the time:

I cannot remember a more dominant F1 design during the end of the '50s and the early '60s than the sharknose Ferraris of 1961. It was one of those seasons when the contest for the Grand Prix World Championship was strictly held between the Ferrari team-mates. Runner-up was for 'all the rest'. The 1961 Ferrari had the necessary power advantage, plus the engine/chassis layout, centre of gravity and weight distribution seemed to be very good. On top of that, the car sounded good and looked great! The Coventry-Climax-powered Lotus in Stirling's, Jimmy's and Innes' hands would still make a virtuoso challenge at the Nürburgring. Siracusa and Rheims were my most memorable races. In comparison the four-cylinder Porsche boxer-powered racing car was reliable and often competitive, but still slightly underpowered. It was relatively big and tall and heavy with old-fashioned brakes and a synchromesh gearbox. I probably learned more about Grand Prix driving from it; that car was more like an anvil than any other Grand Prix car I drove subsequently.

Giancarlo Baghetti, the occasional 'wild card' man on the Ferrari F1 team, which consisted mainly of Phil Hill, von Trips and Ginther, had a very good race going with me in Sicily. As usual in those days, the circuit was quite dangerous and tricky. Beyond the details of the race, Siracusa was just fabulous with Mount Aetna smoking in the background. I recall one day sitting in an amphitheatre constructed out of a marble hillside overlooking the Mediterranean. The acoustics were such that you could overhear a normal conversation from the farthest and highest seats. It gave me a chill to think that the Phoenicians had built it so many hundreds of years before the Romans took over. I will always remember that I got fastest lap there because the organisers gave me one of the most beautiful trophies in my whole collection, a flat gold piece with an engraved racing car to mark 'giro piu veloce'.

Baghetti's performance did not earn him an automatic entry into the Grand Prix team, and there were no team orders for him to appear at Monaco less than three weeks later, although he wasn't left out in the cold. It was not until much later, 1985 in fact, that Baghetti would learn what the 'Commendatore' thought of him; Enzo described him thus in *Ferrari-Piloti, che gente* (1985, p. 276):

> When I met Giancarlo Baghetti, he struck me as a cold-blooded, cautious and reserved young man. But once in a car, he showed his true colours. His career got off to a hugely successful start; the press hailed him as another Varzi. I don't know if this was a factor, but that certainly didn't help him, and his luck began to wane. Then he became a photographer for a magazine which devoted little space to car racing; he once asked me for an interview or 'frank conversation' as they like to call it. I declined the offer, earning for myself on the pages of a high gloss magazine laments for his burnt-out career.

Even Mairesse received better treatment than that eventually, but Enzo Ferrari was not known for his displays of gratitude, at least in the long term, whatever might have transpired in the immediate aftermath of Baghetti's triumph. Baghetti wouldn't be the only Ferrari driver to get Enzo's patronising evaluation in the last years of Ferrari's life. The accuracy of the reference to Varzi is questionable; there certainly didn't seem to be many journalists who made this comparison. In an interview with *Motor Racing*'s Alan Brinton just after the race, Baghetti revealed that he wouldn't be going to Monaco but would be contesting the Naples Grand Prix, another non-championship event, instead. He seemed happy just to be getting some more time in the car. Brinton says that the names Castelotti and Musso were being cast around as figures to compare Baghetti to, rather than Varzi, but Baghetti himself was serious and unassuming.

In the weeks between Siracusa and Monaco, there was much discussion about the outcome in Sicily, and deep regret that the British teams with the FPF Climax engine only producing 140–150bhp were unlikely to be competitive. Now *Autosport*'s editor sounded as if he had shifted his ground, holding the British constructors responsible for not planning for the new formula in the same way as the Germans and Italians. At Silverstone, Moss won the third round of the Inter-Continental series with the Rob Walker Cooper in a fine race. This event also marked the last appearance of a Vanwall, the rear-engined VW-14 with which John Surtees turned in a good performance, as did Chuck Daigh in a Scarab, but these cars were just too late – particularly sad for Vanwall which had been so dominant only a few short years before.

Just after Siracusa, Ferrari sent its main drivers to the Targa Florio, where Phil Hill had a very big accident in the first lap. He and Ginther were out, and von Trips and Gendebien went on to give the 246SP, the rear-engined Dino sports car, its first victory. Baghetti wasn't entered, but a works Testa Rossa was there for Ricardo Rodriguez and Willy Mairesse, and this retired with a fuel leak. However, what the racing world was really waiting for was the first round of the World Championship and the new regulations.

1961
FIRST
CHAMPIONSHIP
POINTS

The Monaco Grand Prix on 14 May 1961 has often been described as one of the great Grand Prix races, and there's little doubt that it was a great event for Ferrari with both the 65-degree engine and the new 120-degree unit putting in superlative performances. If it hadn't been for Stirling Moss, this would have been one of the greatest Ferrari races ever, but there was Moss, shining in his role as underdog.

At the last minute, Chiti and team manager Tavoni were still worried about the 120-degree engine and decided to send test driver Ginther with the new engine (chassis 0001); they were clearly hedging their bets. The entries for Phil Hill (chassis 0003) and Wolfgang von Trips (chassis 0002) had been in for some time. Bonnier and Gurney were expected to be the opposition, their good braking likely to be a bonus at Monaco in spite of the fact that Porsche had retained drums rather than introducing discs. The drum-braked Porsches had surprised a lot of people at Siracusa, though Baghetti was thought to be braking early even when under pressure from Gurney. At Monaco Gurney was in an older car while Bonnier and Hans Herrmann had new fuel-injected engines in newly designed machines (Typ 787).

While Romulo Tavoni stood guard over his three cars at Monaco, proud of the attention they were getting at this most glamorous of circuits, he knew that the Ferraris would have to work hard there. This was the circuit least suited to the car's character – or so he thought. Ginther would have to qualify for one of the sixteen places on the grid, while Hill and von Trips were guaranteed spots. These were the 'bad ole days' of Formula 1 where each circuit and organising body made up the rules concerning how many entries were allowed and how disputes were settled. It was primitive by modern standards, and when the cars were weighed, each team had to declare how much fuel it was carrying so the officials could add that into the total!

As the cars prepared for the first practice session on Thursday afternoon, the serious racing world had its first opportunity to look at the new Ferraris, as well as new cars from several other teams including Lotus with their 21. While there were several detail differences between each of the three Ferraris, the main obvious and outward distinction was in the carburettor coverings. The Hill and Trips cars had a gauze covering over a single large opening in the rear bodywork, while Ginther's car featured two separate openings because the carburettors were further apart in the 120-degree engine. This single gauze covering replaced the Perspex covers used in testing, though the latter would reappear from time to time. On the 120-degree engine, the cylinder heads each had twin overhead camshafts and two plugs per cylinder; Weber 40mm downdraft carbs with triple chokes were mounted on the heads. Ignition was by twin coil arrangement and twin distributors and the 120-degree engine featured a number of details that differentiated it from the 65-degree unit, such as the mounting location and type of fuel pump, which were intended to protect it from engine temperature. Also, the circular type oil pumps were found at the rear of the exhaust camshafts. It was hoped that this revised arrangement would solve the scavenging problems encountered in testing. The same five-speed gearbox was used on both cars with a rear-mounted clutch and inboard disc brakes.

The three Ferraris immediately set a rapid pace; Ginther's speed indicated he would qualify with some ease, and all three were in the 1 minute 41 seconds range, as was Moss after sorting out some fuel feed problems. The pace was affected at first by the fact that the drivers needed to get accustomed to subtle changes to the circuit – the pits had been moved to the side of the narrow 'island' opposite the position they occupy today, and the Tobacconist Corner on the approach to the old pits had

Opposite: Carlo Chiti talks to Phil Hill before practice at Monaco in 1961. Von Trips is standing behind him. The single gauze coverings on the carburettors of the 65-degree engine are evident. (Ferrari Centro Documentazione)

Von Trips's, Ginther's and Hill's
cars line up for practice.
(Jim Gleave/Atlantic Art)

been eased somewhat. Armco barriers had sprung up in many locations
for the first time, reinforcing the use of hay bales if not entirely replacing
them. As Clark and then Ireland found the pace in the new Lotus, so too
did Graham Hill with one of the MkII Coventry-Climax engines, but these
had four cylinders and the V8 was still a long way off. As the Porsches
spent the first session getting suspension settings right, Clark suddenly
put in a wild-looking lap at 1 minute 39.6 seconds and then disappeared
as the Lotus demolished itself against one of the new barriers, leaving
plenty of rebuilding work for the mechanics who had only just completed
the cars.

Those of us who remember getting up for Monaco practice on Friday
might recall the odd feeling we had when the Grand Prix cars went out at
7.15a.m. and we had already been watching Formula Junior since 5.30!
If we had managed to sleep through the 1100cc Juniors, we didn't when
the 1.5-litre F1 cars emerged. First Richie Ginther flew around for the
first of many laps to build up his familiarity with the car and to test its
reliability, and then both Hill and Trips put in fast laps, quicker than
Thursday with no major changes having been made to the cars. Ginther's
1 minute 39.3 seconds made him quickest of all, with Clark's time
remaining second. Graham Hill used the new MkII engine to good effect
to split the Ferraris, but Phil Hill and von Trips looked happy in fourth
and fifth. Jack Brabham had meanwhile departed for Indianapolis to try to
qualify for the 500. Stirling Moss was trying out the spare Rob Walker
car, the Cooper, which was not handling well and was put to one side as

A 65-degree engine car with single carb cover. Note the intakes to cool the rear brakes and the welded chassis tubes. (Jim Gleave/Atlantic Art)

Rear view showing the car's lengthy exhaust pipes with support brackets. Negative camber is apparent even at rest. (Jim Gleave/Atlantic Art)

I have never, ever driven a race as hard as I did at Monaco, at least for a good 90 per cent of it. I'm convinced of it. I'd go around a corner, and if it wasn't quite right I'd say to myself, 'Well let's try to start the perfect lap from here' and then I'd go along and after eight corners, if it still wouldn't be exactly right, I'd say 'OK let's start it from here'. All the time I was doing this to keep myself right on the limit. I was consciously saying to myself I had to stay on the limit. I had the Ferraris between 2 seconds and 4 seconds behind me after I had got past Richie, and that was nothing because every time I went around a hairpin I could see them, and all the time I was thinking they were just sitting there. So I thought, 'Gee, let's see if I can make a car's length', and I'd make a car's length and then the next lap they would take it away and I thought they were just playing with me. I guess Richie was doing the same thing. If I had done my pole time every lap, I would have only been 40 seconds quicker at the end than I was. Richie and I both did the same lap time as it happens, and my whole race was only some 2 seconds quicker than his in the whole 100 laps, so he wasn't hanging around. Phil was also in there for most of the time and I knew that for most of the race.

So the principle of it is that the race is really made by sustaining the maximum amount of speed for the maximum amount of time. It's like saying 'I'm going to run a hundred yards and keep it going for a mile' – it just doesn't happen, but there at Monaco it did. You can't really compare that with the Mille Miglia or some other races, but at Monaco it was clearly closer to the limit than at any other race for more of the time. What counts is the amount of effort and the kind of effort you put in on any one day.

When the race was going on, I didn't see it as 'one of my best', because when you are racing, you are, usually, as fast as you reasonably can be at the time, and it's only when you look back on it and put the whole thing together that you realise you were absolutely flat out. When you are racing you are always trying as hard as you can. All right, in some races, you only try as hard as you can for five laps or ten laps, but over that period you are absolutely on the limit. You are running 10/10ths and you are as near to disaster as you can possibly go. When you are driving like this all your attention is on what you are doing and that doesn't give you time to consider what you are doing, you are just doing it. When you are trying to get a fastest lap, you don't say: 'I am going to get a fastest lap' but instead you go into a corner and you say: 'Right, I'm going to get the throttle down a little bit earlier' and hopefully that will work. Then for the next corner you try to brake as late as you can, and you measure how much later you are braking, and then you put all these things together for a lap, and when you are in a race you are trying to put all the laps together.

My lap record in the Monaco race, which was shared with Richie Ginther, was something like 3 seconds quicker than my pole position time. That was an amazing amount, especially there where you were passing back markers which is always a problem. OK, in those days it was not like now. The cars were relatively narrower for the circuit . . .

you had more room . . . but still if you were trying to pass people like Brabham and Clark it was not easy.

When you are racing, as a driver, you have to know the other drivers and what they are like and their style, their weaknesses and their strengths. If you were going into a corner, you had to have the respect of the other driver, and respect also means that you realise if I am going into a corner neck and neck with you, and I look across to you, you just know that it's my corner and I have to somehow just out-psych you. It might be just something like indicating 'you first . . . your go' and you take them in too deep, which I've done, and they go up the escape road, or something like that. It's different now but it is still respect. I guess looking back at the Monaco race, that process must have been going well because, in retrospect, Richie and Phil and I lapped everyone including Trips who was fourth, and because the average lap time was so quick, all three of us must have been operating at that level of effort.

I think one of my strengths in racing was my braking. I reckoned I could brake later than most people. I would use braking to position the car and if you can use your brakes later than most people and get the car more composed, then that is of greater benefit at Monaco than anywhere else in the whole season. At Monaco you brake reasonably hard into slow corners but just not from very high speed. The difference in acceleration from one car to another is not that much,

Ginther and Moss, and Jo Bonnier's Porsche (2), Monaco, 1961. (Jim Gleave/Atlantic Art)

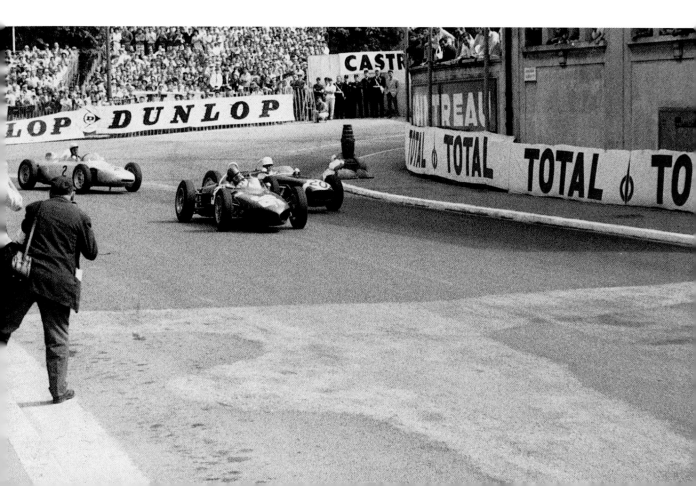

Just behind the lead battle, Phil Hill holds off Bruce McLaren's Cooper and Graham Hill's BRM, exiting the Gasometer hairpin at Monaco in 1961. (Jim Gleave/Atlantic Art)

and in my case in that race I had less than the Ferrari . . . they were definitely quicker on acceleration, but the braking difference was quite a lot. I think my old friend Herb Jones, who I still see, was noting the little differences in the braking each lap. Of course, the two Ferraris were pushing me to do this and that's why it was such a great race.

On lap 14 both Moss and Bonnier nipped inside Ginther, and shortly afterwards Phil Hill pushed the Ferrari past Gurney. Then von Trips did likewise, putting the three Ferraris in line astern in third, fourth and fifth. From laps 20 to 24 the three Maranello cars scrapped among themselves. Phil Hill slipped past Ginther, and all three Ferraris closed on Bonnier's Porsche as Moss pulled away. For lap after lap the Ferraris and the Porsche were within inches of each other, courting disaster but somehow managing not to make contact. By lap 40, Ginther, who had been sitting behind von Trips for some time, forced his way past, caught up with Bonnier, and then made a heart-stopping move up the inside at the hairpin at the end of the lap. Ferrari and Porsche shot past the pits side by side, the Ferrari power showing as they approached Sainte Devote. Ginther was getting his second wind as he set out again after team-mate Hill. Moss's 10 second lead was no longer growing. Ginther, driving brilliantly, was pushing Hill and towing the Porsche, and at half distance, all the lead cars were circulating under their practice times and cutting Moss's lead. A further 5 laps later the Hill-Ginther pace brought the two Ferraris up into Moss's sight. While Bonnier's car expired on lap 60, one of the best ever Grand Prix races was unfolding, with Moss's underpowered Lotus fighting fiercely to stave off the more powerful Ferraris which were flying on a circuit thought to be less than suitable to the character Baghetti had shown the cars to have on the sweeps of Siracusa.

While some reports of the day say Hill and Ginther were not a match for Moss in passing slower cars, in actual fact they managed to keep finding the machines they needed to overtake at just the wrong places and consequently lost more time which they then had to win back. Considering Ginther's limited Grand Prix experience, his driving looked highly impressive to all those gathered within a few feet of the cars as they sped past. Phil Hill talked to the author about the handling of his car during this period:

> I was impressed by the difference in Richie's car and our car, I mean Trip's and mine. The roadholding of Richie's seemed to be considerably superior. To me this wasn't Richie, it was the car. There was no question that anyone who drove the higher cg [centre of gravity] engine later in the season remarked upon it all year long. I don't think it would make much difference, if any, on a very fast circuit but certainly on the back and forth of a circuit like Monaco, the difference was very noticeable.

On lap 75 the diminutive Ginther got past Hill and set off after Moss. Then on lap 84 he set the fastest time of 1 minute 36.3 seconds, not that far off the record achieved the previous year in a 2.5-litre. He was now getting closer to Moss, with Phil Hill hanging on behind him. First Moss and then Ginther's Ferrari lapped von Trips on lap 89, and Ginther, who had been furiously chewing gum the whole race, spat it out. He was obviously getting serious. The Ferrari pits were nearly hysterical and every lap there was a message to Ginther to go faster, to catch Moss, to

Press photographers are hard at work as Phil Hill leads Graham Hill, von Trips and John Surtees' Cooper, Monaco, 1961. (Jim Gleave/Atlantic Art)

give everything – clearly he was doing all of that. The race ran out with Ginther 3 seconds behind Moss, but Hill had fallen further behind. Hill stopped on his slowing down lap to give von Trips a lift back because the number 40 car had had an electrical failure, the first and only sign of Ferrari weakness. According to the Monaco rules, von Trips was classified fourth even though he was not running, rather than down the order behind those who were. These were the days when individual race organisers could impose their own regulations! Even Jim Clark in the Lotus was still running after early mechanical problems had put him eleven laps behind. The points that von Trips earned would mean a lot at the end of the season.

Ginther was quoted as saying he could not have tried any harder and the spectators were in agreement, as all the leaders got a magnificent reception on the slow-down lap. This had been a spectacular success for the 'sharknose', but it hadn't won. Nevertheless, Ginther, quoted by Alan Henry (Henry, 1989, p. 147), said Monaco was his greatest race: 'My car and my effort there were stronger than they were when I won in the Honda [Mexico, 1965] which was just plain faster than its opposition, but at Monaco both Stirling and I were three seconds below the pole time in the race. Staggering, isn't it? I set the lap record very late but Stirling equalled it next time around. That son of a gun! If you did well against him, then you'd really done something special.'

Phil Hill on his own on the straight leading to the Gasometer, Monaco, 1961. (Jim Gleave/Atlantic Art)

Opposite, above: Stirling Moss has just taken the lead from Ginther, Monaco, 1961. Note the removal of the car's side panels to aid cooling. (Jim Gleave/Atlantic Art)

Below: Ginther concentrates on keeping Moss in sight for the next ninety laps. This is on the exit of the hairpin on to Boulevard Albert 1er, Monaco, 1961. (Jim Gleave/Atlantic Art)

Richie Ginther in the Station hairpin at lap 50, Monaco, 1961. (Archive von Trips/Fodisch)

After the race, all three Ferrari drivers reported that the carburettors were flooding after each tight corner, and Phil Hill said that he was beginning to have brake problems because he had been using them so hard. Hill later said (Grayson, 1975) that he was optimistic about the 1961 season after Ferrari's strong start to the year, but there were still problems to be sorted out, such as the amount of cockpit heat drivers had to live with. He also said he would have gladly swapped some of the Ferraris' extra horsepower for the handling of the Rob Walker Lotus, especially at places like Monaco. This all left some work to be done for the next Grand Prix at Zandvoort in Holland only a week later. Some years after, in fact shortly before he died, Ginther recounted how upset he had been that Tavoni had told him to drop back and let Hill and von Trips take up the chase for Moss. It wasn't until lap 70 that the Ferrari pits saw the error and let him go – and then Hill wouldn't allow him to go past. Ginther was not pleased and said: 'I thought we were friends'. Ginther's comment about the car was that 'Monaco was a handling circuit and – compared to the Lotus – the Ferrari didn't handle worth a damn' (*Autosport*, 15 March 1990).

Not all the excitement was happening in Monaco, however. In the early 1960s non-championship races were run in abundance, sometimes even

Von Trips turns into the Gasometer hairpin towards the end of the race, Monaco, 1961. (Gunter Molter)

Moss takes the flag from Louis Chiron, Monaco, 1961. (Jim Gleave/Atlantic Art)

on the same day as a Grand Prix. Such was the case on the Monaco weekend when the Gran Premio di Napoli took place in Naples. While the three 'senior' Ferrari drivers were thrashing away with Moss at Monaco, Siracusa victor Baghetti had been sent to run the F.I.S.A. entry over 1½-mile Posillipo circuit, a tough little street course on the edge of the Italian city. Only a few years before F1 races had taken place in the daunting, up-and-down venue of the city park in the heart of Naples, which was lined with large trees and stone walls.

Baghetti was driving the same car in which he had won his Sicilian victory (chassis 0008) and was looking forward to another strong performance on Italian soil, but he was to get a few surprises before the weekend was over. Although this was not a strong field of F1 cars, it was an interesting race because it included some of the most dedicated privateers in the formula, many of whom were not well known outside their own countries. The British contingent included Roy Salvadori in the Yeoman Credit Cooper, which had failed to get an entry for Monaco alongside John Surtees; Reg Parnell had decided to send the second car to Naples. The other Brits included John Campbell-Jones in a Cooper T51, Keith Greene in the unique Gilby, Ian Burgess in a Camoradi Team entry Lotus 18. Then there was Gerry Ashmore and Tim Parnell, Reg's tall and able son, both in Lotus 18s, a Rob Walker Cooper T51 lent to Italian Giuseppi Maugeri, who had not been allowed to run at Siracusa because he was too slow, Lorenzo Bandini, who looked as if he might be a threat in the Centro Sud Cooper-Maserati, various assorted machines driven by Prinoth, Alberti, Boffa, Natili, and another Emeryson for Andre Pilette.

Like Monaco, the grid size was limited because Posillipo is a tight circuit. Only thirteen cars were due to qualify, disappointing for those who could not even get on to a second-class grid in a second-class race. But at the front of the grid unexpected things were happening, and Salvadori and Baghetti, who had both thought they would be on pole, were taken by surprise by the competent privateer Gerry Ashmore, who ended up in front. Salvadori took the centre spot on the front row and pushed Baghetti down to third.

As the flag went down on the thirteen cars, everyone was amazed as Lorenzo Bandini managed to shove the sizeable Cooper-Maserati through the smallest of gaps and pass all the occupants of the front row. But Roy Salvadori, who felt he had a very good chance of winning this race, and Baghetti were right on Bandini's heels. It wasn't long before both got past. Then Giancarlo Baghetti went into the lead of his second F1 race, and Gerry Ashmore also overtook Bandini. Salvadori recalled the race with both enthusiasm and disappointment:

I was quickest in practice for a while and I thought Baghetti was the only real opposition and he hadn't had much experience. When Baghetti got past, I decided to stay on his tail and give him some trouble, but something was going wrong with the handling. Afterwards I found out that my mechanic saw the tyre going down but he couldn't warn me and I was heading for the pits anyway when I lost it on a bend. I must have been going too fast. I was stuck backwards between two trees but I did get it going again and got back and changed the tyre. I think I eventually finished eighth which wasn't bad, but was a terrible disappointment because we could have won.

Keith Greene had spun the Gilby in an incident that involved both Boffa and Tim Parnell, but Baghetti had pulled away after Salvadori stopped, and had built up a two-lap lead. The danger of relaxing too much soon became clear to Baghetti and presented him with a good learning opportunity: he managed to spin while not pushing very hard on an easy part of the circuit and when he was well in the lead. This happened very near the end of the 62-lap race and allowed Gerry Ashmore to achieve one of his best results, holding second with a disintegrating gearbox and with Bandini storming after him. Ashmore pulled the gap back to one lap, with Bandini in third, Ian Burgess fourth and Roberto Bussinello fifth in a deTomaso-OSCA entered by Isobelle deTomaso. Baghetti had set the fastest lap at only 69.57mph though he had led most of the way.

The Dutch Grand Prix at Zandvoort among the sandy dunes of the Dutch seacoast took place only one week after Monaco and Naples. It was a strange event by modern standards with such a short break between races and only fifteen starters to take the grid on a relatively spacious circuit, but for Ferrari it was an immensely successful race. All three entries were on the front of the grid and the result banished the memories of a circuit that had rarely been kind to Ferrari. It was also the first ever Grand Prix in which every starter finished.

Phil Hill recollected that he had been waiting for Zandvoort because he believed the 'sharknose' would be at its best there. The mid-engined configuration of the new car was eminently suited to the ups and downs and fast bends, and he thought the Ferrari power advantage should really make its presence felt.

Scuderia Ferrari sent three cars to Holland, all of them with the 120-degree power unit. The team also supplied what was described as a brand new chassis for Phil Hill; it carried the same number as his Monaco car, 0003. Denis Jenkinson argued this was not a new car but just the 120-degree engine in the same chassis that Hill drove at Monaco. Nevertheless, a number of subtle developments had been introduced into the suspension, not all of them good, and a lot of time was spent throughout the weekend changing springs, altering tyre pressures, and modifying shock absorber settings. There was an extra difficulty in that practice was restricted to two sessions on Saturday and one on Sunday morning, all counting towards grid positions. This was not the best environment in which to sort out a new car. Wolfgang von Trips did have a new chassis (0004) and Ginther was in his Monaco 0001, but the Ferrari transporter didn't even show up on Saturday until it was time for the second session. It remains unclear why this happened.

Most of the teams didn't like Zandvoort much because the weather was enormously changeable, sand was often blowing on to the track and into drivers' faces, the officials were not the easiest to get along with, and it was often difficult to obtain accurate times. Add to this the organiser's prerogative of offering a two-car entry to a 'local' driver, and it was a recipe for a bad weekend.

The 'local' was the huge and affable Dutchman Carel Godin de Beaufort, a count who ran his own private team called Ecurie Maarsbergen. He borrowed a works Porsche for himself and entered a second for Hans Herrmann, thus giving Porsche the chance to run a total of four cars with which to try to whittle down the Ferrari opposition. De Beaufort was a pleasant character and not a bad driver, though his bulk was certainly a handicap in single-seaters. Roy Salvadori and a few others were annoyed that once again the Yeoman Credit team were confined to only one entry: Surtees in his Cooper.

Without the Ferraris for the first Saturday practice, the other runners were doing their best to build up an advantage, and lap times quickened more rapidly than anybody had expected. Moss had set the record in a 2.5-litre car the previous year at 1 minute 33.8 seconds. There was a surprised response when the 'smaller' cars were the first under 1 minute 40 seconds and then Brabham put in a solid 1 minute 36.6 seconds in the Cooper.

Von Trips, who hadn't been particularly impressive in the 65-degree car at Monaco, began to show some of what many felt to be his true ability by equalling Brabham's time in the Saturday afternoon session. Phil Hill felt the axle ratios on his car were too high but nevertheless put in a good 1 minute 37 seconds time with Ginther in between his two team-mates. Von Trips was reported to have said the Ferrari's handling was 'horrible as usual' (Nye, 1979) but there didn't seem to be much indication of this in his driving: the car cut a path smoothly through the dunes. However, it was still Stirling Moss in the Lotus who was quickest in the session and appeared to provide another threat to the red cars.

A final practice period on Sunday morning saw a number of changes in the Ferrari camp: the axle ratios were lowered; Dunlop 650s were now on the cars; and a number of suspension settings had been altered, presumably introducing more negative camber, which was to be a source of continuing irritation to the Dunlop engineers. The bigger 650×15in Dunlops at the rear went some way to control oversteer and make the back end of the car more stable. The changes gave Hill the first real chance to shine in the 'sharknose' and he set a 1 minute 35.7 second lap, good enough for pole. Von Trips then equalled Hill's time, while Ginther was a bit slower at 1 minute 35.9 seconds. But the Ferrari dream had come true – an all-red front row. Moss and Graham Hill followed ahead of Gurney and Brabham, Brooks, Surtees, Clark and the rest. Formula Junior Lotus driver Trevor Taylor had been moved up to replace the injured Innes Ireland. Clark was still experiencing a number of engine maladies and had not yet begun to shine.

As the cars left the paddock for the 3.15p.m. start on Sunday, the weather had warmed and a number of teams had changed carburettor jets, but special agony had been reserved for the already nervous pole man Phil Hill, who discovered that a pivot pin in the clutch assembly had either fallen or been left out. He had no clutch on the warm-up lap and tore around the circuit to get back into the pits. Tavoni and the mechanics fell on the job in an instant and a replacement was put in, though it was the wrong size and thus not very secure. The organisers had been good enough to delay the start by five minutes so the pole man could take up his place, and *Motor Racing*'s 'Chandos' described Hill as using the delay to 'calm his palpitating heart with his right hand while he unwrapped a stick of gum with his left!' (*Motor Racing*, July 1961). He also describes the relaxed scene – other drivers wandering about, not worried about the delay and making quips such as 'OK, boys, time to get started . . . leave that one at the pits!' Moss was alleged to have said (Nolan, 1996) 'push that thing away, it'll only jam up the rest of us', and when that didn't perturb Hill he added: 'Oh look Phil, they're taking the whole back end out of your car.' According to Nolan, this was supposed to have irritated Hill, and *Motor Racing* did speculate about whether the aggravation at the start put a serious dent in Hill's plans. Hill and Trips were thought to have agreed with the team that whoever got a clear lead would keep it. Hill, however, had hoped for a clearer message from Enzo Ferrari about who was the team leader: 'At the start of the 1961 season there was this awareness that we were not only racing the other teams, but we were racing each other to win a designation as Numero Uno from Ferrari, a promised decision which he nonetheless withheld race after race and, indeed, never did make.' (Grayson, 1975, p. 230). Nor does Hill say much about the race other than that he set out after von Trips but couldn't catch him.

Three Ferraris on the front row of the Dutch Grand Prix in 1961. Phil Hill gets just a nose in front as the flag drops. (BRSSC Archives)

As the flag fell for the 75-lapper, Ginther lost his front row advantage by spinning the wheels far too much and saw Hill and von Trips pull away from him, with Moss doing his best to get between them. Hill shut the door on Moss, perhaps in repayment for the comments on the grid (if they were really made), and held second behind his team-mate. It didn't look as if the pre-race clutch problems were affecting him, though he had lost his pole spot. As the field came around at the end of the first tour, von Trips pulled out a lead on Hill, and Graham Hill's BRM and Jim Clark's new Lotus were chasing Phil, with Gurney, Moss, Ginther, Bonnier and Brabham following.

By the third lap the pattern of the race seemed clear, but Jim Clark was sizing up the BRM and set the fastest lap of 1 minute 35.5 seconds on lap 7. He then passed Graham to take up a serious chase for Phil. All the British cars now had the Climax MkII engine, which had nowhere near the power of the Ferrari; Clark's competitiveness in this race was an indication that he was a very good driver, and that possibly the Lotus 21's ultra-slim design and tiny nose meant it had better aerodynamics than the 'sharknose', which had a considerably larger frontal area. Zandvoort seemed to be saying that the Ferrari needed those 30–40 extra horses to stay ahead of Clark.

After many laps with no change in the order, Ginther lost a few places after his engine started to cut out occasionally, and suddenly Clark made a move that took him past Phil Hill. The Ferrari could, and did, get back past the Scot, but was not controlling the race or protecting von Trip's lead. By half distance, Ginther's engine had apparently improved and he took a few places back, although his seat mounting had broken and he was sliding around in the car on corners. This was a particular problem for Ginther because the cockpit was already pretty big for him. Phil Hill then helped von Trips pull out a 6 second gap on Clark, indicating that perhaps he had been taking it sensibly in the early stages. While Hill and Ginther each had a Lotus hanging on to the back of them, von Trips was easing away, hoping to become the first German to win a Grand Prix since 1939. It also became apparent that there had been no pits visits by the midway mark.

At the two-thirds point Phil Hill pulled away from Clark and in the space of a few laps, closed on von Trips, where he remained until the end in an impressive demonstration of superiority. Richie Ginther, gallantly holding off Moss and still behind Clark, had further trouble when the main throttle spring on the Ferrari broke, and he had to return the throttle pedal by lifting it with his foot. This gave Moss the chance to shoot past. As von Trips took the flag, Ginther did his best to overtake Moss and resume fourth spot, but missed it by less than a tenth of a second.

All the cars that started had finished, and not one car from any team had visited the pits – the first time this had ever occurred. Ferraris were first, second and fifth. For a reason never explained, there was no playing of either the Italian or German national anthems and no post-race celebration. This was presumably due to the vast crowds that swept

Von Trips leads Phil Hill in the Dutch Grand Prix, 1961. (Ferrari Centro Documentazione)

Phil Hill drives Ginther's car in practice, trying to get the right gear ratio combination, Zandvoort, 1961. (Ferret Fotographic)

across the track to the pits. The race just finished and everything fizzled out, but the Ferrari team was very happy. The Dutch win and his recent Targa Florio victory sent signals that von Trips had got his occasional impulsiveness behind the wheel under control and he looked a good bet for the championship, but so did Phil Hill who had always been the more competitive of the two. Moss and von Trips were on 12 World Championship points and Phil Hill had 10.

While the Grand Prix action had been taking place, yet another non-championship F1 race had been run at Crystal Palace in London for the London Trophy. Roy Salvadori took advantage of not being invited to Zandvoort and gave the second Yeoman Credit team Cooper a good win. He had also won three support races and his total of four victories was a good earner for those days.

By 18 June and the third round of the World Championship, there had been two further F1 races and some serious sports car events. The Rand Trophy was more like a Formula Libre race than anything going on in Europe, but the South African race organisations always worked hard to produce good events and the competitors were every bit as serious as their distant colleagues. Syd van der Vyver won the race in his Lotus 18-Alfa Romeo, a car currently racing on the British historic scene. On the same day, Stirling Moss saw off a good essentially British field at Brands Hatch for the Silver City Trophy. Moss was driving a BRP Lotus 18, as was Bonnier, and these had been updated to Lotus 21 specs. Gurney was

Richie Ginther at the 1961 Dutch Grand Prix. (Ferret Fotographic)

also on loan in a Lotus 18. Moss moved ahead of Clark and won fairly easily by 10 seconds.

After von Trips and Gendebien had won the Targa Florio, Masten Gregory and Lloyd 'Lucky' Casner gave the Camoradi Team a great victory at the Nürburgring on 28 May in their Tipo 61 'Birdcage' Maserati ahead of the Rodriguez brothers; Phil Hill had set fastest lap. On 10–11 June the Le Mans 24-Hours saw Phil Hill and Gendebien lead a Ferrari 1–2–3 victory. It was a busy period for professional and semi-professional drivers, as was the custom of the time. Such hectic schedules remained a characteristic of racing up until the early 1970s, 1973 being more or less the last year when every Grand Prix driver entered the big sports car events as well.

As the team transporters unloaded their contents prior to the first practice session late on Friday afternoon, 16 June, there was considerable trepidation in the air. The 14-kilometre Spa-Francorchamps circuit, reaching through the dense Ardennes forest not far from the Belgian–German border, was unquestionably the hardest Grand Prix course anywhere in the world. It swept downhill past the pits and swung upwards through Eau Rouge – still reckoned to be the toughest corner in motor racing – out on to long stretches of public road before dipping into Burnenville. It then went on to Malmedy down the 3 mile 'straight' to Stavelot, where it turned to head back through flat-out sweeps to Blanchimont and the hairpin at La Source. Spa had bitten hard the previous year, injuring Stirling Moss and Mike Taylor seriously and killing Alan Stacey and Chris Bristow.

Four cars were on hand from Ferrari: von Trips had chassis 0004, the same car with which he had won at Zandvoort; Hill had chassis 0003 again; Ginther was in 0001; and there was a fourth, bright yellow 'sharknose' with race number 8 – this was chassis 0002, the 65-degree engine machine that von Trips had used at Monaco. This machine was brought for Ferrari's long-time sports car stalwart Olivier Gendebien, a Belgian, who had just won at Le Mans and earned a drive in the Grand Prix team. Although he was actually entered by Equipe National Belge who also had the two Emerysons there, Gendebien was clearly being looked after by the Ferrari mechanics throughout the weekend.

Cedric Selzer started work as a mechanic for Lotus at the Spa race and looked after Jim Clark's cars for many years. He recalled how impressive the 'sharknose' machines were when he first saw them as a spectator at Monaco, and when Gendebien came past him while he was working in the pits at Spa. He said he was amazed by how striking the car was, especially the Belgian's in bright yellow.

As the machines were readied for practice, the Dunlop tyre technicians under the command of Vic Barlow became very worried about the amount of negative camber on the Ferraris (Henry, 1989; Nye, 1979). Denis Jenkinson took a close look at what was going on. He described the Dunlop technicians as 'sucking their thermometers and worrying about the temperature of the rear treads' because of the degree of camber (*Motosport*, July 1961, p. 547). Apparently, Barlow managed to convince Chiti that the inside edges of the narrow tyres were doing too much work and he thought they couldn't take the strain, especially with the sustained high speeds of Spa. When the mechanics finally took some of the camber off and the cars went out to practice, the handling was actually better. The Zandvoort set-up would have been far too severe for Spa. This showed the degree to which Ferrari were still learning about rear-engined cars, in spite of the fact that the drivers, especially Phil Hill, had already been pointing out this particular problem.

For the first practice, all the main Climax-using teams and even some of the privateers like Jack Lewis had the newer engine. Bandini was driving a new Cooper, still with the Maserati engine. The first session was marred almost immediately by Cliff Allison, who was involved in a serious crash at Blanchimont, writing off the UDT Lotus and hurting himself sufficiently to end his career: he had broken his legs again, repeating his Monaco injury of 1960. Allison's accident caused a resurgence of interest in roll-over hoops – his had folded back over the engine. He had been thrown out and the hoop hadn't helped him much. The concern was that if it had folded forward it would have trapped him in the car. The Grand Prix Drivers' Association had recently been formed, with Moss as President and Bonnier as Vice-President, mainly with the intention at looking at safety and circuit issues; at this stage anti-hoop opinion was very strong.

Phil Hill, von Trips and Gendebien were quickly on the pace in the early laps, though Richie Ginther was slower because he had never raced at Spa before. By the end of the period, von Trips was quickest, and the

Ginther's car at Spa, 1961.
(Graham White)

Ferrari's power was more evident than it had been in previous races. Even Gendebien spent some time at the top of the list in the car with the older engine, but von Trips was quicker still. On Friday no one lapped in under 4 minutes and most cars were a full 14 seconds off Brabham's record of 3 minute 50 seconds, set the previous year with an additional litre. On Saturday, everyone was faster, and the BRMs of Graham Hill and Tony Brooks suddenly looked as if they might challenge the Ferraris by getting down to the 4 minute 7 seconds bracket. However, at the end of the period all the four 'sharknose' cars were out on the track, and there was some slipstreaming going on to pull them away from the field, but it came as a big shock when the times were published. Phil Hill, who 'missed' the signal to come in and did another lap, registered the only sub-four minute lap in 3 minute 59.3 seconds with von Trips $\frac{3}{10}$ second behind. Surtees was on 4 minute 6 seconds and Ginther a fraction behind. Graham Hill was a somewhat shocked 1.5 seconds adrift of Ginther.

Nearly 30 seconds separated Phil Hill in his well-deserved pole position from Lucien Bianchi in the Lotus 18 at the back. The Ecurie National Belge had withdrawn the Emerysons, which frankly were falling apart, and made a deal to borrow the cars of Tony Marsh and Wolfgang Seidel who were, like Bianchi, in Lotus 18s. These were promptly and hurriedly painted yellow for Mairesse and Bianchi, who were allowed to use times achieved in cars they were not going to race! There were some who hoped for rain just for the chance of seeing the paint get washed away.

Just before this book was completed, the author had the chance to talk to Stirling Moss again, this time about Spa and what it was like to return there after his experience in 1960. His diary carries a very short comment about the 1961 Spa race: 'car fair, SM fair'. He started eighth and finished eighth, and admitted to 'probably taking it easy'. Jackie Stewart had once said that anyone who said they enjoyed (the old) Spa was either lying or crazy. What was Moss's view of going back there for that 1961 race?

Spa was a circuit that when you finished a race there it was the most exciting race you'd done. When you're doing it, it's the most fearful thing you're doing. You go down that Masta straight and you come to that kink, and you wonder where do you back off. There is a tremendous exhilaration you get through there. All the time you know it is dangerous but you also know that is what sharpens it up. Having said that, it was not my favourite race because it was dangerous. Because I'm considered a pretty quick driver I had to go bloody close to the limit there and that frightened me. But, it was such an enormous buzz when you'd done it, that you deserved to be there. But 1960 had demonstrated just how dodgy it was. When I went back in 1961 I just put it out of my mind. That's how I got round these things. Sometimes I'd notice that there would be a smell of grass. Then if there was an accident, I'd think 'Christ, that's the smell of death' and then you might smell the same thing another time and think 'God, there's something wrong'. You can't afford that. You just can't afford to allow that to happen. I think people like Stewart would accept the dangers and then try to lessen them, and I would say 'I don't want to face it'. I'm prepared to look the other way . . . which is pretty stupid now that you think about it.

In the race, all thoughts of the danger seemed to evaporate as the pack went tidily down the hill and away out into the country. The weather was overcast but dry, and the expected Ferrari train arrived back on schedule with Hill in the lead, followed by Gendebien, Ginther and von Trips. They played with each other a bit and Gendebien came around in front to the great delight of the crowd, but Hill soon took command. Von Trips took up station just behind him and that was how they carried on for thirty laps, or 423 kilometres. Ginther moved into third and the Belgian settled for fourth, but it was a staggering 1–2–3–4 performance. Gendebien had developed an oil leak which was throwing up a fine spray and had been slowing him down, and Phil Hill had warned the Belgian about it before he went past and disappeared.

Surtees was almost a minute adrift in fifth, ahead of the Porsches, whose early season threat seemed to have stalled. Towards the end, privateer Jack Lewis had towed around behind the Ferraris to ninth, and Ginther grabbed fastest lap at 221.676kph, some 131mph. In the process of doing this, Ginther rapidly caught his team-mates again, and was clearly learning the circuit very quickly. Had he been the one to get the good start, it might well have been his race, but Phil Hill led home a

Gendebien in practice at Spa in 1961 in chassis 0002, the 65-degree engine car. (Jim Gleave/Atlantic Art)

Von Trips in practice at La Source hairpin, Spa, 1961. (Jim Gleave/Atlantic Art)

crushing Ferrari team. Most of the British runners ran into one kind of trouble or another, the common theme being that the pace was just too much for the Climax engines. Even a brief shower of rain towards the end didn't slow the race by much.

The championship points tally now stood at 19 to Hill and 18 to von Trips, with Moss and Ginther sharing 12, and Clark on 4. The situation didn't look good for anyone not driving a Ferrari, and the *Autosport* editorial roundly turned on the British constructors for not having the foresight of Enzo Ferrari who had faced up to the implications of the regulation changes. What the editor probably didn't know was that sentiment within the Ferrari team wasn't quite so upbeat, and both Hill and von Trips must have been wishing even harder for either Ferrari himself or Tavoni to dictate a policy on team orders. With the cars as quick and as close as they were, there was going to be some close in-fighting.

Two weeks after Spa, all the teams made their way to another circuit that was bound to suit the power of the Ferraris, the flat-out blind and wide open spaces of Rheims-Gueux. East of Paris in the champagne country, the circuit had been the sight of some historic battles in the past, many of which had featured Ferrari, and had also included Ferrari fighting Ferrari.

SEFAC again took the decision to send a team of four cars; and while the fourth machine – for two-time winner Giancarlo Baghetti – was nominally entered by F.I.S.A. and its constituent Scuderia Sant. Ambroeus, it was more than evident that chassis number 0008 was a works car

Hill leads von Trips on the approach to Stavelot corner, Spa, 1961. (Paul Meis)

Ginther under braking for Stavelot, Spa, 1961. (Paul Meis)

Phil Hill leaves La Source for the last time to win the Belgian Grand Prix, 1961. (Jim Gleave/Atlantic Art)

in everything but name. Baghetti was said to be relaxed, but he must have felt the responsibility of now being on the grid with the three 'regulars'.

Spa winner Hill had 0003 again, this time carrying race number 16, and von Trips had his usual 0004 as race number 20, with Ginther again in 0001, race number 18. Rumours of a Syd van de Vyver-built 1.5 Alfa Romeo Giulietta engine for Stirling Moss in the Rob Walker Lotus had been circulating, but these appeared to be untrue when the Rob Walker team appeared with the usual choice of Lotus and Cooper, each with the Climax engine. The rest of the grid was more or less as usual, with considerable despondency among the teams about what the Ferraris might do to them. While no further moves towards nominating a number one driver had been made at Ferrari, there were several 'insiders' who felt that von Trips had got the nod, and Phil Hill was looking more worried than usual. There was some surprise at Baghetti's appearance, as most people thought his 'arrangement' was for Italian events only and he was making his non-Italian debut. He wasn't overwhelmed by the occasion and took himself off to see the sights of Rheims between practice sessions.

Practice was held from 6.30p.m. on Wednesday, Thursday and Friday in an attempt to avoid the enormous heat, which reached 96 degrees in the shade with a track temperature of 126 degrees on race day. It seemed strange to hold practice so late in the day if the race was going to be in the heat of the afternoon, but as many said, 'this is France'. However, the French organisers had accepted a larger, 26-car grid so there wouldn't be the usual fighting to qualify.

Phil Hill stamped his authority on the first practice session in a thoroughly masterly manner. He used his supreme skill on high-speed circuits to demoralise the opposition, not by a fraction but by a full 1½ seconds. It is ironic that Enzo Ferrari's later dismissal of Hill's talent should have been on the grounds of what he was so good at: 'He wasn't an exceptional, top-flight racer, but he was dependable and profitable mainly on high-speed circuits. He preferred wide curves and long straight-aways to winding roads, the so-called demanding circuits which require constant driving precision.' (Ferrari, 1985, p. 257) Enzo Ferrari was the master of the 'back-handed compliment'.

However, before Hill put in his pole-position lap, von Trips had been registering good times, getting down to 2 minutes 26.4 seconds but without realising for some time that he was providing a very nice tow for Stirling Moss. Von Trips' response when he saw all the waving from Tavoni in the pit and noticed Moss still stuck to his tail was not to slow down, but to go faster for the rest of the lap in a vain effort to get away. Moss was happy with the resulting 2 minutes 27.6 seconds time, which he acknowledged he never would have achieved without the Ferrari's help.

The author is again grateful for Stirling Moss's habit of keeping a very detailed diary from early in his racing days. From the 1961 journal he read his comments on the Wednesday practice:

In the first practice the car was geared to 161mph at 8000rpm. I can get 7500 or 7600 on my own but 7900 if I'm behind the Ferrari! It was at 7200rpm at the rise on the straight, 7600 with the Ferrari at the same place, that's another 400 revs behind the Ferrari, Trips I think. The car handles badly due to the rear suspension. Phil Hill did 2.24.9. Trips 2.26.4, so Hill had a big lead, and Ginther 2.27.4, I was 2.27.6, Innes 2.30.2, Graham Hill 2.29.1 and Clark 2.30.3, Baghetti 2.30.9, Brabham 2.31, so in other words I was reasonably up there.

Ginther had got down to 2 minutes 26.8 seconds, and this meant three of the Ferraris had detached themselves from the rest of the field, except for Moss in the Rob Walker Lotus who was a bit closer – and he still had a gap on everyone else. Aside from Baghetti, who needed to familiarise himself with the high-speed bends of this ultra-quick course, the rest of the Ferraris could have skipped the rest of practice because they had set their grid times. In fact, Hill and von Trips did sit out Thursday, but Hill's lead seemed to provoke a degree of dissatisfaction in von Trips in his own car, and the intra-team rivalry began to intensify.

Phil Hill later wrote that Rheims provided an incident which revealed the kind of childish behaviour competition could provoke (Grayson, 1975). Hill admitted to a 'guilty surge of pleasure' over the gap he had over von Trips, but he had noticed that von Trips was talking to Tavoni, presumably complaining about his car. At the beginning of the season, the drivers had agreed not to ask to drive each other's cars, such was the concern at what each might do to the other's machine. But von Trips was pleading for Tavoni to drop the rule, not so he could drive Hill's car, but so Hill had to drive von Trips's. Hill didn't want to because there was a risk he would find a fault and it would get repaired and put von Trips on an equal footing. However, just as this discussion was going on another driver came in and said there was oil down at the Thillois corner. Hill decided this was an excuse for a slow lap. Though von Trips's car was a bit down on power, the difference was minimal, and Hill drove a lap just a shade slower than his own and quicker by a second than von Trips. There didn't seem to be very much oil at Thillois so he then did three very hard laps. He came in to a dispirited von Trips and said the car seemed fine but he couldn't do a really fast lap because of all the oil! To rub it in even further, Hill had won the 100 bottles of champagne awarded for fastest lap.

It was during this Thursday's practice that Ferrari tried some experiments on Ginther's car, which had the two Perspex bulges over the carburettors. These had been used in the last few races instead of the fine gauze covers. For a few laps number 18 went round with what was a huge air intake for the time, bolted on to the tail section and extending all the way up to the top of the roll-over bar behind Ginther's head, bringing air directly into the carbs. As times were not affected, the device was soon removed and never seen again, but of course such intakes returned to almost all single seaters later in the decade.

With Hill and von Trips giving the second session a miss, Ginther was quickest. But the period was notable for a near-disaster when a black Peugeot with Paris plates pulled out on to the circuit and drove in the wrong direction towards Thillois at the top of the straight as Baghetti braked for the corner with Bruce McLaren in his Cooper tucked in behind him in order to try to get a tow down the straight. They both had to leave the track up the escape road at the corner to avoid a huge accident, and the police took the offender away for questioning.

Both Ginther and Baghetti had been the target of virtually all the other drivers who were trying to catch them for a tow, but Tavoni, Chiti and the mechanics continually warned the two Ferrari drivers so they could avoid this – not an easy prospect for Baghetti who was still trying to learn the circuit and doing this well with a time of 2 minute 30.8 seconds.

In the final practice on Friday, Hill and von Trips did a few laps, and Ginther secured his front row spot with his team-mates, but Baghetti was still down in twelfth, which gave a little hope that Ferraris weren't all-conquering. As it turned out, this was a false hope. Saturday was a free day, and most attention was focused on finding ways of keeping the cars cool on what was another very hot summer's day.

On Sunday, the hottest day of the week so far, the 7 kilometre Rheims public road circuit sparkled, or perhaps simmered, as the 2.30 start drew near. The circuit – essentially a triangle with three very fast sections of public road – had been in use since 1926. It had been the scene of some of Grand Prix racing's most heroic battles, including the contest between Hawthorn's Ferrari and Fangio's Maserati in 1953, and between the Lancia D-50s of Collins and Castellotti in 1956 – both races where the finishers were less than a second apart. But on this occasion, the high temperature meant the tar was melting, and it had been rutted by the preceding Formula Junior heat. Course officials covered the mess with loose gravel and some more tar in a vain attempt to repair the surface for the Grand Prix. Phil Hill compared it to driving on ball bearings.

The French Grand Prix official starter was the unpredictable and rotund Toto Roche, who said he would drop the French flag any time after the 30-second board had been shown. First the 1 minute board was up, followed 5 seconds later by the 30-second board, followed 9 seconds later by the starting flag!

With many cars stripped of body panels to aid cooling, and the three works Ferraris reverting to gauze coverings for the carburettors rather than Perspex, the field was off. The red cars on the front row went as one, and more or less stayed as one for the first four laps until Ginther got caught out by the melting surface down at the Muizon hairpin which leads on to the longest straight. He slewed sideways, enough to let Moss, who had been making the most of the slipstream, past into third and forcing Surtees in his Cooper to take avoiding action into the bank.

A lap later Hill and von Trips were pulling away and Moss was third, but Ginther was setting about trying to catch him. There had been several pit visitors with damage and overheating problems, and there was a big gap between the leaders and a huge battle between Clark, Ireland, Graham Hill, Baghetti, Bonnier, McLaren and Gurney. These drivers were to run nose to tail for many laps. Baghetti was getting the racecraft training of his life and holding his own. For some reason, Moss had been given fastest lap on the second tour – almost certainly incorrect, as the Ferraris were moving away from him at the time. Ginther went up to third on lap 6. Denis Jenkinson reported that Ferrari team orders issued at

Opposite: Richie Ginther prepares for Thursday's practice for the French Grand Prix at Rheims with the first attempt at ram air effect. It was soon removed. (John Godfrey Collection)

Phil Hill is caught on camera at Rheims, with Carlo Chiti to the left. (Author's Collection)

Opposite, above: Hill, von Trips and Ginther at the moment the flag falls to start the French Grand Prix in 1961. All three spin their wheels. (Ferrari Centro Documentazione)

Below: Ginther leads Hill and von Trips just after the start of the French Grand Prix, 1961. (Author's Collection)

the start were that Hill was not to win, so he seemed determined to at least show how far out front he could be when he relinquished his spot to von Trips. He had a 2 second lead on lap 10, with Ginther 18 seconds further back and Moss 6 more seconds in arrears, but the big battle behind had Baghetti towing the others closer to Moss. Baghetti even had Ireland briefly on the grass at the Muizon hairpin.

The action got even hotter as Hill let von Trips past on lap 13, and Moss was slowing. He told the author: 'I had a rear brake pipe go which was hit by a stone, and I kept going for some laps but had no brakes at all and then lost 12 minutes getting it fixed.'

A strange set of signals came out to the leading Ferrari pair on lap 15 saying 'GINT'. It was unclear whether this meant to wait for Ginther or to let Ginther past, but the sign reappeared, followed by a 'slow down' signal. On the twentieth tour Phil Hill came around on his own and von Trips coasted into the pits, a stone having holed his radiator, overheating the engine and causing the first engine failure of the season. Because the cars had been running within their limits, this was particularly galling to von Trips. The worries about the 120-degree engine had been put aside and the units had been performing faultlessly.

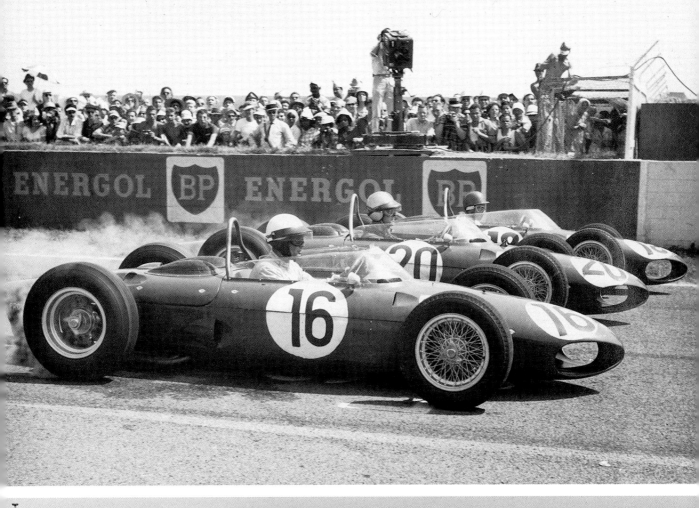

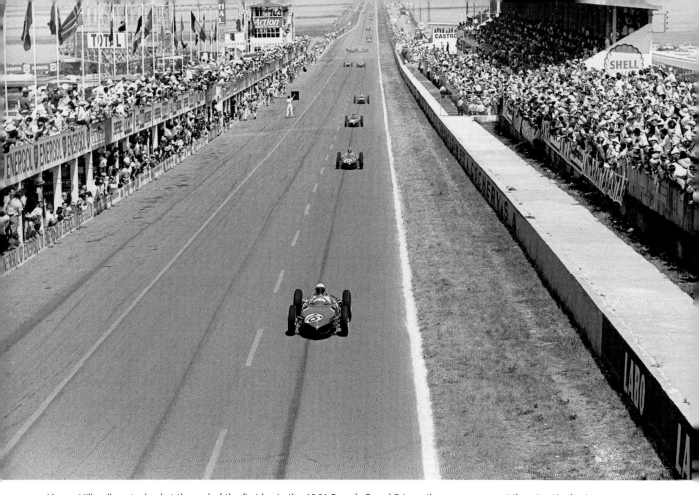

Above: Hill pulls out a lead at the end of the first lap in the 1961 French Grand Prix as the cars come past the pits. (Author's Collection) *Below:* Hill stretches the lead on lap 2, French Grand Prix, 1961. (Author's Collection)

Hill was still some 10 seconds ahead of Ginther, and this remained the position for many laps, with the big battle taking place with the Clark/Ireland Lotus attack on Baghetti, now in third. Ginther had another off-road excursion but held his place; Brabham retired, as did the wildly driven Porsche of de Beaufort who frightened a lot of people, Brabham especially. Roy Salvadori recounted that, having finally gained entry into a Grand Prix, he was 'running around out there on my own, missing all the action, but I finished eighth'. Between laps 35 and 40, Clark, Gurney and Bonnier took turns roughing up Baghetti and leading him, but each time he regained his position. Then in the mêlée Clark got hit by a stone, dropped back and couldn't catch them again. However, on lap 38, a real drama occurred. Ginther came past the pits on his own, and there in the distance up at the exit from Thillois was Phil Hill pointing the wrong way. Moss had been following the Ferraris after three stops and was many laps behind. Moss said: 'I was following Phil and he spun and hit me.' Talking to the author, Hill said he finished ninth not because he had a spin but 'because Stirling Moss hit me'. In fact, as Hill recounts (Grayson, 1975, p. 230): 'I was leading and all I had to do was stay pointed in the right direction. Then near the end of the race I spun at Thillois and Moss, who also lost it, clouted me and my engine stalled. The starter wouldn't work. I tried to push start it. It got away from me and ran over my leg. Finally, I did get it going but I was two laps behind everyone. My golden opportunity to make a decisive leap in the point standings was lost in one stupid move.'

Von Trips – a study in concentration at the right-hand corner after the pits, Rheims, 1961. (Author's Collection)

Above: Richie Ginther on the straight, French Grand Prix, 1961. (Author's Collection)

Right: Hill in his typical upright position, French Grand Prix, 1961. (Author's Collection)

Opposite: The battle for the lead, Rheims, 1961: Bonnier (10), Gurney (12), Ireland (6), Baghetti (50) and Bruce McLaren (4). (Author's Collection)

Ginther passes Lucien Bianchi having a spin at Thillois on the melting road surface, Rheims, 1961. (Jim Gleave/Atlantic Art)

Ireland (Lotus) leads Graham Hill (BRM) and Baghetti, Rheims, 1961. (Author's Collection)

Baghetti pursues Tony Brooks (BRM) in the early laps, French Grand Prix, 1961. (Jim Gleave/Atlantic Art)

Asked at which race the 'sharknose' had felt the best that season, Hill said it was at the French Grand Prix, so this mistake was even more painful: 'I just gave away nine points. My car was at its best there. I had over a second in qualifying, that's when I took Trips's car out and there was supposed to have been oil there which I didn't see, but I didn't tell Trips that.' A quick laugh follows this last comment, but the memory of being stuck in the middle of the road having lost the lead was clearly still a sharp one.

As Hill was desperately trying to get restarted, in spite of a recent FIA rule which had forbidden this, Moss pulled in to retire. But the high drama was not over: on the next lap Ginther stormed into the Ferrari pit with faltering oil pressure and signalled for a top-up, but another new rule outlawed this practice and Tavoni sent him away. Ginther just managed to hold his lead with Baghetti and the two Porsches closing, Gurney actually moving into second. Next time around Ginther pulled over at the hairpin because the oil pressure was gone. As Baghetti came flying up to the corner, he suddenly knew what was happening because he had seen Hill stopped for over a lap.

There were eleven laps to go to the end of the forty-seventh French Grand Prix. For nine of these, less than half a second separated the Italian from the American Gurney and the Swedish Bonnier in the two silver Porsches. First Baghetti led, then one or both of the Porsches, and several times they came past the pits three abreast. With two laps to go, Bonnier was the first to succumb, the engine smoking, but he was sent

Baghetti remained close to Bonnier and Gurney during the final few laps at Rheims in 1961. (Ferrari Centro Documentazione)

out again by his pit to finish. Gurney came past for the 51st lap alongside the Ferrari but inches in front. Then Baghetti re-passed at the back, only for Gurney to seize the lead at the Thillois corner and head down the final straight in front. Some 300 to 400 yards before the finish, the Ferrari emerged out of the slipstream and Baghetti surged ahead to become the first driver ever to win his first Grand Prix, eclipsing the monumental drive of Mike Hawthorn at the same circuit eight years earlier. A demoralised Phil Hill brought Ginther back on the tail of his car at the end of what was clearly one of the hardest Grand Prix races ever.

The World Championship points table didn't change much, but Baghetti was suddenly on it with Dan Gurney. Baghetti had driven in three Formula 1 races and won them all. Sadly, he wasn't going to win another. However, some years later, Baghetti reflected on the French race, recalling that he had driven up to Rheims with his brother in their Giulietta Spider, and that on the first evening Hill, von Trips and Ginther 'talked about the difficulties of driving at Rheims, and offered help and advice'. He also remembered getting Mauro Forghieri, 'a newly recruited young engineer making his Formula 1 debut', into trouble with Chiti.

Baghetti closes on Gurney two laps from the end of the 1961 French Grand Prix. (Jim Gleave/Atlantic Art)

Baghetti comes into the pits having taken the flag at the French Grand Prix; the shadow in front of the car is Tavoni's. (Raymond Jenkins)

Forghieri received a violent dressing-down from Chiti because Baghetti had urged him to take some time off and go for a swim. He also recalled that the cars were carrying a thermos of fresh water each, but at a stop his had got fuel spilled into it. He didn't know this until he tried it! He had to go to the victory dinner in a shirt and pullover because he hadn't bothered to bring a dinner jacket. He really wasn't expecting to win (*Ferrari World*, September/October 1991).

Dan Gurney also reflected on that race, reminding the author that it, along with Siracusa, had been one of the more memorable events:

At Rheims Baghetti and I had another good race. Coming out of the last corner I thought I had won it, but then he got by me in the last metres of that long straight, a famous pass that has gone down in Grand Prix history, my Porsche being no match for the beautiful sharknose from Maranello. Baghetti and I later kidded each other about the outcome of the race, and I got the impression that he was almost a bit embarrassed by the surprising dominance of the Ferrari. He seemed to be calm, patient and unruffled by the challenges mounted by the other makes. He did a damn good job too, and I was sorry to see that he did not get the chance to race more that season.

1961
THE TITLE BECKONS

Aweek passed and the fourth round in the Inter-Continental series took place at Silverstone for the British Empire Trophy. Even though Stirling Moss won after driving almost the entire distance without a clutch, the *Autosport* editorial was now virtually ringing the death knell for the 2.5-litre series, having championed it months earlier. The race was notable for the appearance of the clever 2.5-litre version of the Ferguson P99, a four-wheel drive car which was to have a limited though short-lived success. Jack Fairman retired it at Silverstone. A day later at East London, South Africa, Syd van de Vyver won the Border 100, again using his Lotus 18-Alfa to good effect, against a fairly unimpressive field.

For the Royal Automobile Club British Grand Prix on 15 July, all the teams headed to the north-west of England and Aintree, and to a much kinder climate than had prevailed at Rheims. There was, at least among the optimists, some hope in fighting the Ferraris on a track that the

Phil Hill's 0003 in the paddock at gloomy Aintree in mid-July 1961 for the British Grand Prix. (Michael Lindsay)

'locals' knew better, but not many bets went as far as the bookies at this great horse-racing venue.

Virtually the whole field was as it had been at Rheims, except for the fact that most of the teams had repainted the cars which had been battered by the French stones. The Ferrari drivers were all in the same chassis that they had raced in France, except Baghetti in 0002 this time entered by Scuderia Sant Ambroeus, though this fact seemed to matter less and less as the season went on. With the title chase still as close as it had been before Rheims, the pressure was on Hill and von Trips to try to build up a lead. Only three championship rounds remained after Aintree. All the 'sharknose' team had reverted to Perspex covers for carburettors in the full expectation that there would be rain.

Ginther, left, and Hill with friend at practice for the 1961 British Grand Prix. (Jim Gleave/Atlantic Art)

Opposite: In the Aintree pit lane, with Baghetti (his back is to the cars) and mechanic Giulio Borsari (in a cap). (Jim Gleave/Atlantic Art)

The significance of Aintree for Ferrari, in addition to its potential impact on the intensifying championship contest, was that the race was run in the wet though practice was dry. The cars had not been tested in the rain, and Baghetti had no experience of the wet at all. Added to this, Aintree was a new circuit for all the Ferrari squad. The grid was spiced up a bit by the appearance of the four-wheel-drive Ferguson P99 in 1.5-litre form, run by the Rob Walker team, and this was now the only front-engined car in F1.

With a stiff wind blowing for the first of two timed periods on Thursday, the Ferraris of Phil Hill and Ginther were at the head of the list: those who had hoped the Ferrari drivers' lack of familiarity with Aintree would be a handicap were quickly disappointed. Bonnier and Ireland were next but no one was under 2 minutes. In the second session, the three works Ferraris were on 1 minute 58.8 seconds, as was Bonnier, but this was partly because the organisers were using stopwatches that only measured to a tenth of a second rather than a thousandth. Stirling Moss ventured out to try the Ferguson and was 1.6 seconds slower than his Lotus; he found the handling was twitchy, but the potential was clearly there.

It poured with rain for both Friday practice slots, so the Thursday times had to stand. Von Trips and Ginther were going quickly in the treacherous wet conditions and Hill, von Trips and Ginther topped the tables in the second rainy session, Hill showing superb car control. Moss in the Ferguson had been stunningly quicker than anyone else in the first session, with Roy Salvadori second, using some new development wet tyres from Dunlop: they would provide a good weekend for Roy. The only notable occurrence in practice involved Baghetti, who was not very happy in the conditions. He made a huge spin at the Melling Crossing esses and struggled to find his way across the grass areas again; he and Tavoni were later summoned to the Clerk of the Course for a talking to.

Clouds gathered for the Saturday afternoon start, and spots of rain caused serious anxiety about whether to use the new high-hysteresis Dunlop wets. With fifteen minutes to go, the clouds opened up and everybody went for wets because there were certain to be pools of water around the circuit. The big grid of thirty cars disappeared off into a ball of spray, to appear a few minutes later with the works Ferraris in charge – Hill followed by von Trips and Ginther. Bonnier, who had done the same practice time as Hill, had been on pole because he achieved his time

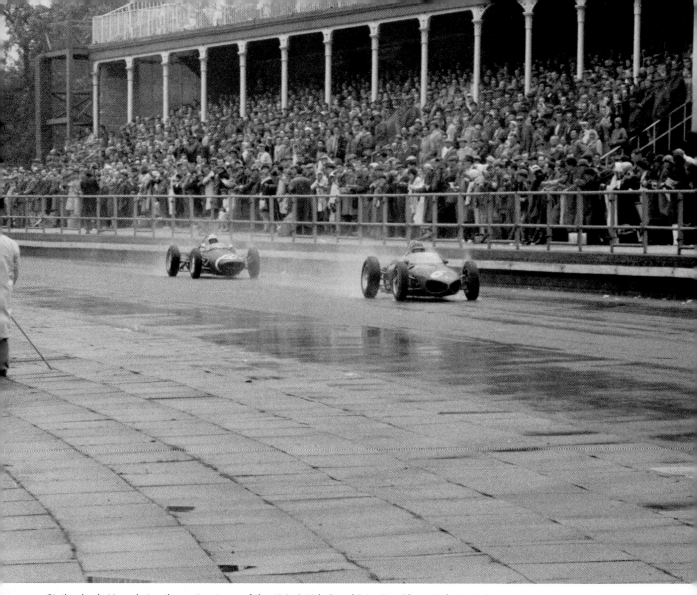

Ginther leads Moss during the wetter stages of the 1961 British Grand Prix. (Jim Gleave/Atlantic Art)

Ginther peers out from under his visor towards the end of the race. (Michael Lindsay)

Von Trips heads for victory as the track dries out at Aintree, 1961. (Archive von Trips/Fodisch)

before the Ferrari, but the Porsche would not handle in the wet and he was struggling. Surtees was once again the victim of an early barging match; Ireland spun and Natili's Cooper broke. After half a dozen laps it was only Moss who could stay with the Ferraris; he passed Ginther, while Phil Hill in a superb demonstration of wet-weather driving was moving away at the front. Then Hill got balked as he came up to lap Keith Greene's Gilby, giving von Trips the chance to get past, and a few laps later the same thing happened to Moss. It was then von Trips's chance to shine in the wet, and Moss couldn't get by. Hill hung on behind with Ginther fourth. Henry Taylor had a bad crash and was being attended to on the circuit; this accident helped him make the decision to retire at the end of the year.

Moss had a big spin on lap 28, allowing von Trips to get further away, and while von Trips was lapping Baghetti, the Italian also lost it and flew backwards through some stout fences, damaging the car but not hurting himself. Hill made a half-spin which allowed Ginther by. Soon, Moss was having a similar brake failure to the one he had experienced in France, Ginther moved into second and Hill took third.

Hill described his excursion in the wet as 'horrifying' after he lost grip in the deep water and headed for a thick wooden upright at the Melling Crossing. He was immensely relieved when the tyres found some grip again. Tony Brooks was a lap down in his BRM, but was going as fast as anyone when his electrics dried out. Ginther allowed Hill by into second and the Ferraris ran out the final half of the 75-lap race at a reduced pace, thus taking the fourth Ferrari victory in a row. The constructors' title was all but guaranteed, although the drivers still had everything to fight for. Porsche, Lotus, BRM and Cooper now knew that the 'sharknose' was as quick and almost as dominant in the wet as it was in the dry. It would take something special to stay on terms with the Italians, and Stirling Moss seemed the only driver who could put up a reasonable threat – and he was in a year-old car.

Two races were run a week later on 23 July; the first was the non-championship Solitude Grand Prix in Germany, another brilliant race, with Innes Ireland's Lotus beating both Bonnier and Gurney by less than 0.2 second. Ferrari decided not to contest this round and prepared instead for the German Grand Prix instead. In the South African F1 series, Bruce Johnstone took his Cooper-Alfa to victory in a very small field at Lourenco Marques, Mozambique, the second event that day. A week later Ernie Pieterse won the Rhodesian Grand Prix at Belvedere in the Heron-Alfa. Both of these races had several Alfa-engined runners; this had become regular practice with the increasing availability of Giulietta engines, which could either be bored out from 1300cc or sleeved down from 1600cc.

The German Grand Prix, scheduled for 8 August at the Nürburgring, marked the first appearance of the new Coventry-Climax V8 engine. No one would quote horsepower figures but it was thought to produce at least 170bhp, still short of what Ferrari could clearly generate. The engine was fitted in Brabham's Cooper, though many aspects of the V8's design had apparently not been taken into account by Cooper, which had to work hard to get the engine and new exhaust layout into the chassis. Cedric Selzer, former Lotus mechanic now working on Clark's car, recalls the appearance of the V8 Climax as the 'beginning of the return' of the British cars.

Ferrari, whose Romulo Tavoni had revealed that all the 120-degree engines had been damaged at Rheims and required major rebuilding for Aintree, brought the usual three cars to Germany for von Trips, Hill and Ginther. Chassis number 0002, last used at Aintree by Baghetti, who damaged it, was repaired for this race, but it was not Baghetti who was picked to drive. Instead, Ferrari sports car and front-engined Grand Prix driver 'Wild Willy' Mairesse was brought into the team as a works entry. While no one actually said that this change had been made because of Baghetti's crash, it was at least implied. It was a strange decision because if crashing was a 'bad thing' in the Ferrari camp, Mairesse didn't seem a very logical choice!

The 1961 German Grand Prix is often singled out as one of the all-time great drives, although perhaps not quite on a par with Fangio's race there in 1957 in the Maserati 250F. Stirling Moss does indeed see it as one of his best – and he had some good ones in 1961 – but it doesn't rank quite as high as Monaco for sheer effort and strategy required. Moss's win, however, has always overshadowed Phil Hill's mastery of a circuit where Enzo Ferrari would later say he hadn't performed that well. Moss's victory disguises not only Hill's efforts but also to some extent the

skill of von Trips, who drove some magnificent laps and completed a thoroughly competent race. Ferrari's unwillingness to name a number one driver by this stage in the season kept the competition very close, but nearly had disastrous results.

Thirty cars practised on the old, 22.8 kilometre circuit in the heart of the brooding Eifel mountains. It was the first time the race had been held there in three years; it had been run at Avus in 1959 and on the Ring's shorter South Circuit in 1960. The record here was Moss's, achieved in the Vanwall back in 1958 at 9 minute 9.2 seconds and with the long 3 mile return section. There were some people who thought this time could not be broken, but there were a lot more hoping to see the first sub-9 minute lap of the twisting, turning and leaping German track.

The first of the two Friday practices was mainly a matter of acclimatis-ation for most teams. Bonnier, who had been testing the Porsche which was in need of some serious development, was quickest, followed by Brabham, Moss and Phil Hill. Brabham was in a Cooper with a four-cylinder engine because the V8 had suffered a distributor drive failure when it was started. Von Trips had an engine failure, the first in practice that season, so a change was being made for the afternoon. The process of swapping the Dino 156 engine is a difficult one and the mechanics didn't manage it on time. In the afternoon, Brabham tried the V8, which was grounding on the bumps of the Ring, and Phil Hill had a hard time controlling his car because the suspension at both the front and the back could not cope with the conditions. The limit of travel was being reached with the result that the car was unstable and bounced about. Hill was working overtime to match Bonnier, finally going a second quicker. According to Hill himself when he later reported it to Denis Jenkinson, he then put together a near-perfect lap and turned in a staggering 8 minute 55.2 seconds time. He described this as a 'freak' that he wouldn't be able to repeat. Alan Henry's account (1989) argues that Hill was out on Dunlop's sticky wet tyres: when they got properly warmed up, they produced a fantastic qualifying lap. Bonnier was a full 9 seconds slower and Clark a further 4 seconds behind. These three were the only drivers under 9 minutes and 10 seconds. At this point von Trips had only done 9 minutes 23 seconds, and Mairesse was a second faster than Ginther but 20 seconds slower than Hill. Several reports describe Hill arriving back in the pits 'stary-eyed and trembling' or 'glassy-eyed', and this was no surprise.

Phil Hill practises for the German Grand Prix, 1961. (BRSCC Archive)

There was a brief unofficial session on Saturday morning so Brabham and von Trips could have some more time. In the official slot Brabham set the quickest time of the day in 9 minute 1.4 seconds, 0.3 seconds quicker than Moss whose third gear kept jumping out. Von Trips did a 9 minute 5.5 seconds lap. This left an American, an Australian, an Englishman and a Swede on the front row of the four-by-three grid. They were driving a Ferrari, Cooper, Lotus and Porsche respectively.

There had been a shower at midday on Sunday but the sun was shining as the 2p.m. start neared. The Dunlop engineers had told everyone who had been using wets to remove them as the track dried. The Ferrari and Porsche teams did, in spite of Hill's previous performance in the dry on the high hysteresis wet tyres, but that had only been over one really hard lap. Moss and the Lotus works team had used the tyres at Solitude in the dry and thought they didn't seem to suffer from the wear that the manufacturers feared. Lotus decided to keep the tyres on.

As the grid departed, the regular watchers were shocked to see Brabham put a Cooper into the lead for the first time that season, and the hopes for the Climax V8 were momentarily high. But poor Brabham hit a damp patch after Hatzenbach, not far out into the country, and the wet spots, like those under the trees at Hockenheim today, were potentially lethal. Brabham, always prepared to poke fun at himself these days, though not so much then, spoke to the author about the short race:

> Well, the new engine was looking pretty good although we were worried a little about whether it would over-heat, but it felt good and I could get away from the others, but I hit this wet patch. Well, I had only had time to put wet tyres on the front when I saw what Moss and the others were doing but I had dry tyres on the back, and they wouldn't grip on this patch, and the car turned and went through a hedge. I was driving along this hedge and I thought maybe I could get out again but there was a ditch there so I couldn't. I think people saw the hedge shaking from the other side as I was driving along it, but I just couldn't get out.

By the fifth of the fifteen laps Moss was pulling out a lead of up to 10 seconds on Phil Hill. Von Trips was starting to catch Hill following several very quick laps, and he was going faster than Moss. Moss was following a similar strategy to the one he had employed at Monaco, using every opportunity to pull out even the tiniest margin. Moss described his approach to the author, working from the memory of something he has clearly gone over many times, rather than his diary account of the race:

Von Trips in the Karussell, 1961.
(Paul Meis)

Von Trips near Hohe-Acht, German Grand Prix, 1961. (Paul Meis)

Phil Hill manages to check his mirror in the Karussell, 1961. (Paul Meis)

Ginther seems to be adjusting something which is not on the steering wheel with his right hand, Nürburgring, 1961. (Paul Meis)

At Nürburgring it is essential to get out around the back quickly, so if you can hold the car on or near the limit, you know you can hold it there on the slightly easier corners. It's so difficult to do, but if you get the car located right for the first of the corners then you feel better as you get to each corner after that. Nürburg is a very rewarding circuit for the purpose of feeling the car. You do it at Monaco in quite a different way. At Monaco, the rewarding thing is that the people are so close, and there are so many corners, but at Nürburgring which of course is much longer and has 176 corners a lap, when you go past the start–finish line and go around the back, it's like going into the countryside. You've got the leaps where if you can hold it flat, you get the adrenalin rush and you feel this is terrific. From that moment the car fits and it's just like putting on a shoe, and it's doing just what you want it to. At that race at the Ring in 1961 I had managed to get a good start and I went around the back where you get a pretty difficult part and I managed to pull away. I remember thinking all the time 'My God, they're going to get to the straight' which is something like 2 miles or so long and 'they're going to come roaring past and I've got to build up everything I can in this bit'. I can say I really worked terribly hard up around the Karussels and I couldn't truly see the cars. And then I got on to the straight and went over one slight brow and I still couldn't see them. Then I went down and up the next hill and I could see they were there. They were coming up and I thought 'My God there's not far to go, maybe a mile or so and then I'm going to be back on my territory where I could really use it.' They would close up again, but it wasn't nearly so urgent. Their proximity to me was a mental problem. As I went round the loop past the pits to turn back towards the country I could see them coming down the straight and I knew it was Hill or Trips, one of the Ferraris, but the Nürburgring isn't the sort of circuit where there are many places where that happens. That's about the only place. It wasn't that big a lead. On the straight, for instance, we were doing about 155, 160 miles an hour – so that's about 250 feet a second, nearly 100 yards a second. Well, 4 seconds and they're quarter of a mile behind or so, and that's meaningful on that circuit. Then just before the end, it started to rain which was a great help. I had started on Green Spots which were really wet tyres and Dunlop tried to talk me out of it and I wouldn't let them. Dunlop's manager talked Jack Brabham into changing his rear wheels which didn't do him any good either, and they said to me 'If these tyres go, they're going to burst on the straight' and I thought 'Oh sod that'. Then of course it was getting quite serious when the treads were getting low and I thought 'Are they going to last?' The sprinkle of rain helped it a lot, and it dropped the temperature.

In spite of Moss's watchful eye, the two Ferraris were gaining on him. After several fast laps, von Trips went past Hill, setting a new official lap record of 9 minute 1.6 seconds in the process, but on lap 11 Hill repaid the compliment, did an 8 minute 57.8 seconds tour and was back in front, drawing closer to the leader. Thousands were shouting for the lead trio at this point, but as Moss said, the rain started, which made it easier for him, and he went out in front by 15 seconds. Mairesse had worked his way up into sixth position but crashed with two laps to go, although he was under no pressure. Ginther was struggling in the conditions, but on the final lap Hill led as they came up the last long straight. As Moss was taking the flag, the two Ferraris, side by side, both hit a large puddle off line and went sideways. It was von Trips who got the car straight first and headed over the line in second, with Phil Hill 1 second behind.

Hill virtually dismisses all his achievements in this race with the comment, 'I screwed it up' (Grayson, 1975, p. 231). In discussion with the author, Hill was slightly more forthcoming. He acknowledged that the chassis seemed to be working well by that point in the season: 'The chassis was adaptable to those very different circuits. It was very good by then.' Hill said there had been little testing of the cars at this period and the developments consisted mainly of 'always meddling with the suspension. We did our best so we didn't have that wear to the inboard edge of the rear tyres. That was always the problem. The Dunlop people were very upset with us.' Asked if Chiti was failing to improve the car during the season, Hill was clear: 'I don't think so. He was steadily improving it. Of course, the others were catching up all the time.'

Jim Clark had driven a hard race to come in fourth in the works Lotus, with Surtees in the Yeoman Credit Cooper and McLaren in the works Cooper next, the Porsches in trouble, Ginther in an uncharacteristic eighth and Mairesse in the bushes. There had been some serious questions asked about the selection of Mairesse. He had been lucky to be supported by the French Ferrari importer Jacques Swaters early in his career and had driven well in the Tour de France in a Berlinetta in 1959; and he won the Tour the following year, which earned him three drives in the F1 team in the front-engined Dino, and subsequently a number of sports car drives. But he was always wild and erratic, and more than once was 'spoken to' at meetings of the Grand Prix Drivers Association. For 1961 he had been in a Lotus 18 and a Lotus 21 in Grand Prix races while also struggling with the hopeless Ecurie National Belge Emeryson-Maseratis. In spite of losing a constructors' point for Ferrari, however, he would be forgiven, he would come back – and he would win, a fact that no one would ever have predicted.

Ferrari now led Lotus by 14 points in the constructors' championship, while von Trips had pulled out a 4-point lead over Phil Hill and Moss was on 21, 8 behind Hill. Ginther's hopes, if he ever had any, were over and the title was clearly going to go to Hill or von Trips after the remaining two races. With five of the eight Grand Prix races counting towards the championship, von Trips was the mathematical favourite, based on the belief that Ferrari would go to Watkins Glen after Monza. Phil Hill's only real chance of taking the championship lay in his winning at Monza and von Trips not scoring.

Many of the teams and drivers rushed back to Brands Hatch for a round of the Inter-Continental Trophy, where Brabham finally secured a win from Clark after Moss's gearbox broke. There was over a month's break until the Italian Grand Prix at Monza on 10 September, and several other races were scheduled in the interval. The Rand Winter Trophy at Grand Central in South Africa was the last event to be held there –

Ginther again in chassis 0001,
German Grand Prix, 1961.
(Paul Meis)

Willy Mairesse trying very hard as
usual, German Grand Prix, 1961.
(Paul Meis)

A rear view of Mairesse in the 65-
degree engine car, chassis 0002,
Nürburgring, 1961. (Paul Meis)

Kyalami was about to be built. Syd van der Vyver won again in the reliable Lotus 18-Alfa Romeo. Then there were two races in Scandinavia. Stirling Moss, in spite of commuting back and forth to the UK for the Tourist Trophy, won the Kannonloppet at Karlskoga in the UDT/BRP Lotus from the back of the grid. Motorbike star Geoff Duke had a serious crash which ended his hopes for a four-wheel career like Surtees'. A week later the Danske Grand Prix was held at Roskilde, a circuit of less than 1 kilometre. Some big names appeared, with Moss taking all of the three heats and Ireland, Salvadori and Henry Taylor following on aggregate. Henry Taylor was making a return after his big shunt at Aintree but was talking about retirement. Brabham, Clark and de Beaufort also came to tackle the little track and its four hairpin turns.

A week before Monza, the traditional Gran Premio de Modena took place, an event with a history that goes back to before the Second World War. Ferrari felt that the race was too close to the significant Grand Prix at Monza and stayed away, although von Trips had taken third in the rear-engined prototype at Modena the previous year when it was an F2 race. Ferrari were also busy doing development work on a chassis for Indianapolis in 1962. The car is thought to have resembled the Grand Prix machine. Enzo Ferrari was reportedly looking for an American Indy driver to pilot it, having seen the adverse affect the Indy efforts were having on Jack Brabham's season. Moss won yet again at Modena. Taking on a good field, he beat the Porsches of Bonnier and Gurney, and Clark's Lotus.

The British motoring press carried stories about Chiti's latest developments which were believed to include fuel injection for the 120-degree engine and a desmodromic valve actuation, as well as titanium connecting-rods and an anti-lock braking system.

An entry of thirty-seven cars was received for Monza; thirty-three showed up and practised on the combined road circuit and banked track, which the British teams had boycotted the previous year because they felt it was too dangerous. The fact that it didn't seem so dangerous this year was perhaps an indication of how quickly things change in motor racing, and the irony is that the banking did not turn out to be the danger spot that year. Spectators visiting Monza today still go around for a glimpse of the steep banking, which was constructed in 1955 on this 10 kilometre high-speed racing circuit. They have trouble envisaging the combined layout, however, as today's very wide pit area and straight were divided into two sections in 1961: the cars coming off the road circuit would run closer to the pits but parallel to the cars coming off the banking and heading down to the Curva Grande to commence a lap of the road circuit. The two 'lanes' were divided by plastic cones!

In the huge and varied field, Brabham's Cooper was again fitted with a Climax V8, and another arrived for the Rob Walker Lotus 18 driven by Moss, while in the back of Graham Hill's new BRM was the team's own brand-new 90-degree V8. Sadly only one of these three V8s would be healthy enough to enter the race. The remainder of the field consisted of all the works teams, semi-professionals and amateurs in every 1.5-litre Grand Prix car that could be found. There were three deTomasos, two with four-cylinder OSCA engines and Vaccarella's car with a Conrerobuilt Alfa Romeo Giulietta engine with twin plug head. Brian Naylor brought his JBW-Maserati, and Maserati engines powered Coopers for Bandini and Trintignant. There was a Lotus for Gaetano Starrabba, and numerous other Lotus 18s, as well as the Emeryson-Climax for Andre Pilette – the only car to fail to qualify.

Enzo Ferrari had a few surprises in store for the rest of the field when the transporter was unloaded. Following the Nürburgring, there had been some testing at Monza during the rest of August in readiness for the team's home Grand Prix. The first surprise occurred when not four nor five but six 'sharknose' cars rolled out into the Monza paddock. Phil Hill was in 0002, the car Mairesse had driven in Germany but now fitted with the 120-degree engine, von Trips was in his usual 0004, and Ginther in 0001. A slight surprise was the reappearance of Baghetti in Hill's regular 0003, this time not entered by F.I.S.A. but by Scuderia Sant Ambroeus. The original prototype 0008 was on hand as a spare. Finally, the development that stunned everyone was the last-minute signing of the nineteen-year-old Mexican Ricardo Rodriguez, who was assigned 0006, another new chassis but with the 65-degree engine.

Ricardo and his 21-year-old brother Pedro had been surprising experts with their driving skills since 1955 when they moved from riding motorbikes to driving cars in Mexico. Their first international events were in the USA and Nassau in 1957, and they had since raced several times at Sebring and Le Mans. Their big events had been sports car races, almost exclusively for Luigi Chinetti's North American Racing Team (NART). Chinetti, of course, was Ferrari's first importer for the USA. While the brothers were both exuberantly fast – Ricardo was usually the quicker – and had won some important races in Nassau, their first major victory was yet to come. They had been fastest at Le Mans in June but then retired. The force behind the brothers' racing was their father Don Pedro Rodriguez, who paid the bills so NART would provide the rides. The self-made millionaire spent every penny on getting his sons to the top in racing, and eventually Chinetti approached Enzo Ferrari about Formula 1 drives for the pair. Ferrari was happy to take them both on at a price, but Pedro stood down, supposedly for 'business reasons', late in 1961 when the Grand Prix opportunity came.

A long-time Rodriguez family friend, Victor Manuel 'Flacco' Barrios, had accompanied the family on many of their first ventures out of Mexico in the early days, and he was on hand when Ricardo showed up at the Modena test track a few days prior to the Grand Prix to 'see if he was capable of driving an F1 car'. He drove under Chiti's gaze only for a few perfunctory laps, and then went off to sign with Enzo Ferrari. Barrios recalled Ricardo receiving the gold medallion from Ferrari: Ricardo was 'relaxed' about the meeting, being much more interested in getting to the circuit for practice. The medallion resides in a box in the home of another family friend in Mexico City, a small reminder of Ricardo's big impact on the Scuderia Ferrari at Monza. Barrios also remembered that Fangio was present during this period and at a dinner in Milan the famous driver told Ricardo that he thought he would win the next year's World Championship.

'Flacco' Barrios, friend of the Rodriguez family, with the 65-degree car tested by Ricardo Rodriguez before the Italian Grand Prix in 1961. This photograph was taken by Ricardo. (Author's Collection)

The Monza lap record stood at 2 minutes 43.6 seconds; Phil Hill had done 2 minutes 41 seconds the previous year in the front-engined 246 Dino, and in the run up to the Grand Prix the Ferraris were running in the 2 minute 46 seconds bracket. There were three and a half hours allocated for first practice on Friday afternoon, but the organisers had also provided some unofficial time on the banked section of track for those who hadn't driven it before. Brabham had Cooper's sole V8, while there were now two new BRMs with V8s. The Rob Walker Climax V8 was installed in a totally revised version of the team's spare Lotus 18. The BRM V8s didn't get much use in practice – one had been damaged and the other was being 'saved'. The author talked to Tony Brooks about what turned out to be his penultimate Grand Prix, and he was less than complimentary about the BRM:

Well, I finished fifth in the race but what I remember is driving a completely uncompetitive car – the BRM – on a great circuit. It had always been a happy circuit for me. I'd won there in 1958 and had fastest lap in 1957, so to be driving this not-even-glorified go-kart there, well it was pathetic, and I was pretty frustrated. That's my memory of the race, and of the whole season really. The reason I drove the car was that the one that won the championship in 1962 driven by Graham Hill was supposed to have been available to us at Monaco in 1961. In fact, what they cobbled up was an overweight BRM with a second-hand 1.5-litre Coventry-Climax engine with about 140 horsepower. It was just pathetic and was one of the things that made it easier for me to retire. That was the P48/57 but it really wasn't worth giving a number to. It was just a bodge-up because they hadn't got a proper car ready. I don't remember running with the Ferraris. The BRM wasn't fast enough to do that. I worked my way up and it was flat out all the way round, but pathetic is the word that springs to mind whenever I think of that BRM. The best thing that happened all season for Hill and myself was my third place at Watkins Glen in my very last race, and fastest lap in the British Grand Prix in the wet. You might ask if it was a heap, how was it fastest? But it was wet, that was all, so it gives you a chance, even with a heap like that.

Clearly, Brooks didn't like the car.

In the Friday practice, only a few cars got out to see how they would work in the race because the rain began to fall, and this meant that only Ginther, Rodriguez, von Trips and Hill put in respectable times. Coming

No. 6 is Ginther's car with a 120-degree engine. There are fewer scoops and air intakes than on the T-car, the original prototype 0008. (Gunter Molter)

The T-car showing Ferrari experimentation with cooling flaps for the radiator and the cockpit. (Gunter Molter)

Ricardo Rodriguez in practice in an F1 car for the first time. (Raymond Jenkins)

off the road portion of the circuit into the South Turn, Rodriguez slid the car from lock to lock on the watery and greasy surface, totally relaxed and at ease; in contrast, Baghetti was showing his discomfort in the wet again. When the circuit dried towards the end of the day, Tavoni kept both Baghetti and Rodriguez going round and round in their own cars and in 0008, the 'training' car. Rodriguez, however, had already had some Monza practice back in May when he co-drove an Alfa Giulietta SZ with Luigi Taramazzo in the Coppa Ascari, so he was feeling very much at home. According to William Nolan (1996), Rodriguez managed to crack the chassis of 0008 during all the thumping around the banking.

With the British eight-cylinder cars encountering a variety of problems, the Ferraris were mostly in a class of their own. Though Graham Hill did get in one lap at 22 minutes 48.7 seconds, only the Ferraris were also under 2 minutes 50 seconds. Many teams were still trying to get used to the banking and the effect it had on the cars. Tim Parnell recounted his experience to the author:

Of course we were on the crazy circuit which included the oval and a lot of people were very sceptical about the oval because it was very, very bumpy and the Grand Prix cars at that time weren't very strongly built cars for the 1.5-litre formula and a lot of people had suspension problems and things like that. I was driving a Lotus-Climax and Jimmy Clark and Innes and Moss were as well. There were a few more . . . Masten Gregory and Henry Taylor.

As all the British V8 runners were getting ready to go back to four cylinders, with the exception of Jack Brabham, the Ferraris were packing up early – von Trips had put in a splendid 2 minute 46.3 seconds lap and then Rodriguez went round in a stunning 2 minutes 46.4 seconds. Ricardo had only been in a Grand Prix car for a matter of days and was now on the front row for the Italian Grand Prix, a tenth of a second slower than von Trips, the most likely contender for the World Championship. Phil Hill remembers Rodriguez' performance but also his irritation at his own situation; he had gearbox problems on Friday and then engine trouble on Saturday. A new engine was finally fitted for him before Saturday was over. This provided some hard work for mechanics Pignatti and Marchetti. If circumstances had been different, he would have expected to go faster, especially at Monza. As it was, von Trips was only half a second quicker than Ginther, and nine-tenths of a second ahead of Hill. With the title at stake, Hill was feeling the pressure and this made him even more concerned about the state of his equipment.

The heat on the Sunday of the race was oppressive, and numerous efforts were made to add further cooling to the cars and the drivers. The

The Ferraris slipstreaming each other at Monza, in 1961. Hill is in front. (Archive von Trips/Fodisch)

Ricardo Rodriguez and his car before the start of the Italian Grand Prix, 1961. (Ferrari Centro Documentazione)

Ferraris appeared with their lower engine panels removed. Moss had been loaned Ireland's Lotus 21, which was thought more likely to threaten the Ferrari than the old Lotus 18. Whether this was Ireland's idea or a Team Lotus gesture is unclear. The Ferrari also went on to the circuit with a higher axle ratio and thus a high first gear. This meant they were likely to be slower off the mark in order to take advantage of the high speeds the race was likely to produce. It also meant the opposition might well get among them.

That opposition was Jim Clark as the English pre-war driver Lord Howe dropped the Italian flag for the start. The Ferraris bogged down slightly before Ginther was away, though it was Rodriguez who got his nose in front for a moment, and then the entire pack disappeared in a din. The cynics were of the view that the two-by-two start was agreed on to keep the non-Ferraris from grabbing a slipstream right away. If that were true, it didn't work, and as they came around the first time, Phil Hill had pushed to the front ahead of Ginther, Rodriguez, Clark, Brabham. The slower-starting von Trips was sixth, and then came Baghetti. The second pack was just adrift of the first seven, and von Trips was trying to get back on terms with his team-mates, going past Clark on the straight and aiming to stay ahead as they turned into the Parabolica right-hander. But Clark had pulled out of the slipstream.

The story of what happened next has been told many times, usually with the core of the tale the same and sometimes with the details changing, but the most plausible account is that von Trips didn't realise Clark had stayed with him as they went for the corner. As a result, they touched wheels and both cars immediately flew out of control, Clark's hitting the banking on the left and coming to rest on the grass left of the track, while von Trips flew up along the spectator banking, whipping along the packed fencing. He was thrown out, as the car rolled and landed in the middle of the circuit. Von Trips was lying on the edge of the circuit; he had been killed instantly. Clark never spoke publicly about the accident, though the Italian courts treated him as the guilty party for some time; his long-time girlfriend Sally Stokes, now Sally Swart, confirmed that it was one of the incidents he never mentioned. However, Clark did describe the accident in his statement to Dr Gatti Edoardo, the Deputy Coroner. This statement was made at 7.30p.m. on 10 September:

Opposite: Overhead view of von Trips's car, Italian Grand Prix, 1961. (Gunter Molter)

The Ferrari team in the Monza paddock. (Gunter Molter)

A pensive von Trips about to go out on to the grid, Monza, 1961. (Raymond Jenkins)

Carlo Chiti attends to Giancarlo Baghetti, Monza, 1961. (Raymond Jenkins)

Rodriguez (8) just gets the jump on von Trips (4) ahead of Ginther (6) and Phil Hill (2) as Graham Hill (24) gets wheel spin on row three alongside Baghetti. (Archive von Trips/Fodisch)

Today I was driving a Lotus car in the Grand Prix of Italy with the number 36. At approximately 250 metres before the Curva Parabolica my Lotus car which was travelling alongside on the left of a Ferrari driven by von Trips was struck by that Ferrari as it moved to the left. At this time we were both travelling at a speed I would estimate to be 140 miles per hour. From the moment of impact, I have no recollection of what happened to my own car or to the Ferrari. My first recollection after the accident was when I found myself still seated in the car which had come to rest on the grass verge on the side of the track. Mr von Trips was a good friend of mine and I am deeply distressed by this accident. (Fodisch and Louis, 1998, p. 111)

Roy Salvadori told the author that he had a strange memory of the accident: he had been in about mid-field and saw the cars flying off the road ahead of him, but he always remembered the accident as happening on the right side of the road – clearly the reverse was true. Jack Brabham was trying not to get too involved in the tussle at the front when the crash happened. He questioned whether it was just the cars driven by Clark and von Trips that touched, suggesting another might have moved over and squeezed von Trips, and the finger has from time to time been pointed at Ricardo Rodriguez. 'Flacco' Barrios was watching from the inside of the circuit at the time of the accident and said that Rodriguez was only inches in front of von Trips but there was no way of knowing whether they had touched. Jim Clark's mechanic, Cedric Selzer, said there was never any doubt in the minds of the Lotus team: 'Clark had out-braked von Trips into the braking area of the corner and von Trips catapulted himself off the wheel of the 21.' There are pictures of Clark helping to move the Ferrari off the circuit, and of the following cars threading their way through the wreckage.

Eleven spectators and von Trips were dead in the worst postwar racing accident since the Le Mans crash in 1955. Three more spectators would die of their injuries; between forty and fifty had been hurt.

Brabham and Baghetti were right behind von Trips and Clark and were lucky to avoid them. The rest of the field came upon the chaos quickly. Baghetti told Graham Gauld some years later that 'when von Trips came to the Parabolica, he braked, but Clark didn't expect him to brake so early and realised he was going to ram von Trips. Clark couldn't move to the right because I was there so he tried to go left and the nose of his Lotus touched the tail of von Trips's car and it flew off' (Gauld, *FORZA*, June 1998, p. 56). Masten Gregory hit some of the debris and the incident contributed to his eventual retirement, but the others got through. None of the drivers appeared to be aware of von Trips's body on the side of the road and they never wanted to talk about it. Only Tim Parnell vividly recalled the impact of seeing the dead being lined up along the bottom of the grass bank during the next few laps.

The Italian Grand Prix continued, however, with Hill, Ginther, Rodriguez and Baghetti leading. Jack Brabham gave them a good race for

Lap 3 at the Italian Grand Prix and Hill leads as the cars driven by Clark and von Trips lie on the grass. (Eoin Young)

Hill (2) looks over at Ginther (6) as Rodriguez (8) and Baghetti (32) follow in the early laps. (Archive von Trips/Fodisch)

at least a few laps, the V8 Climax seeming to have got the measure of the Ferraris. For some ten laps the order remained pretty much the same; then Brabham dropped away as his engine overheated. The only real close battle was further back for fifth and sixth between Moss and Gurney. The two BRMs were going well, though a long way back, until Graham Hill's blew up. Jack Lewis in his private Cooper moved up the field from his sixteenth starting position and eventually reached fourth place. On lap 13, the 'sharknose' quartet, which had been cruising steadily with either Hill or Ginther in front, suddenly broke up as first Rodriguez and then Baghetti pitted. Baghetti's car retired immediately with broken valve springs, though he had set fastest lap as early as lap 2 with a time of 2 minutes 48.4 seconds, an average speed of over 213kph or 132.8mph. The Rodriguez car was checked over front and rear, the oil level being tested more than once, and the story released was that the fuel pump had failed. However, more serious engine trouble was the likely cause, as the less powerful 65-degree engine had been staying with 120-degree cars for the entire distance.

Rodriguez' departure from the fray meant that he was no longer in a position to support Phil Hill. According to 'Flacco' Barrios, Ricardo had told him on the Saturday night before the race that Enzo Ferrari wanted Ricardo to help Hill, because if Hill could win the World Championship, it would have a positive impact on Ferrari sales in America. This conversation was alleged to have taken place either just before or just after the drivers' meeting. According to Ricardo, von Trips said that he would win because it would be good for Ferrari in Germany. Barrios said that those privy to these conversations went away feeling that if von Trips had not crashed, he would not have carried out these alleged orders. It is not known what Enzo Ferrari really wanted.

Just as Tavoni had got over Rodriguez' failure and slowed Hill and Ginther, Ginther started to drop back and the flying Moss began to catch him rapidly. By the time Ginther's engine had expired like his team-mate's, Moss was making up the gap. Hill held on to his lead, though there was concern in the Ferrari camp that if Hill's engine went like the others, Stirling Moss would move into first position in the World Championship. However, fate wasn't kind to Moss in his last full year as a Grand Prix driver: the Lotus's wheel-bearing broke on lap 37 and he was out. With Gurney now 30 seconds behind, and McLaren, Lewis and Brooks further back, Phil Hill crossed the finish line as the first American ever to become World Champion.

Hill had been unaware of the seriousness of von Trips's accident. He had been in front of it when it occurred and most of the remains of the cars had been cleared the next time around. Hill knew that von Trips had recovered from earlier big shunts, and it was only as he got back into the Ferrari pits and spoke with Chiti that he understood the severity of what had happened. Hill described the aftermath:

I was told Ferrari had watched the race on TV and that when Ginther, Rodriguez and Baghetti went out and Trips had crashed Ferrari had said 'Abbiamo perduto. We have lost.' But I won. And I won the championship, which was a warming relief, a soaring feeling. But it was to be a short flight. When the race ended, I asked Chiti about Trips. He muttered something but I could tell from his face that it was not the truth. I suspected the worst, but it was not until after champagne and congratulations on the victory stand that I was told. Fourteen spectators had died as well. (Grayson, 1975, p. 231)

A number of important events took place in the aftermath of the Monza crash. First, and not surprisingly, the Italian press hunted around for a scapegoat; Jim Clark fitted the bill. He was indeed charged with manslaughter, though this charge was soon dropped. The Vatican raised its voice and criticism was directed at Enzo Ferrari for building the car that had killed the spectators. This provided Ferrari with one of his many opportunities to act the injured victim, and he announced that the team would not be going to Watkins Glen for the US Grand Prix on 8 October. To some people he presented the image of a man in mourning for his lost driver. Brock Yates argues this was unlikely to be the truth and that 'Ferrari mused with a priest with whom he maintained a close friendship "I think I did a good job faking my sadness for the death of von Trips"' (Yates, 1992, p. 340). Jack Brabham, among others, was adamant that if the blame were to be laid at anyone's door, it should be placed firmly with the organisers, who had been advised several times about the danger to

Phil Hill, 1961 World Champion. (Archive von Trips/Fodisch)

the public in the approach to the Parabolica. Denis Jenkinson, a shrewd observer on many issues, was of the view that the accident was 'totally unforeseeable'.

It is likely, and reasonable, that Ferrari made a pragmatic decision to rest on his laurels after Monza. After all, the team had won the constructors' championship: it had 40 points after Monza and Lotus only had 24 – the British team could only get another 8 points for a maximum score at Watkins Glen (and they did). This was the period when only the top finisher for each marque scored points. Phil Hill had taken an unassailable lead in the drivers' title chase with 34 points; von Trips had 33, and Moss and Gurney 21 each. Ginther was fifth in the standings with 16 points, Baghetti was ninth with 9 and Gendebien thirteenth with 3. Ferrari's decision, of course, meant that the new American World Champion would not get to race in his own country. It seems this was not something that Hill ever complained about.

There is little evidence that Enzo Ferrari ever showed any particular gratitude for what Hill had done. Hill 'confessed' later that he was feeling somewhat sorry for Ferrari for the treatment he was getting in Italy, particularly because he knew the criticism about the cars was unjustified – Ferraris were being built very strong. It was at this time, in later September 1961, that Hill went to visit Enzo Ferrari at his home in Modena, and Ferrari asked Hill if he would stay for 1962. Hill said he would, not knowing at this stage that not only were all the key figures at Ferrari on the verge of leaving, but Enzo was also arranging to see both Stirling Moss and John Surtees about driving for the Scuderia, or, in Moss's case, at least driving a Ferrari in Formula 1.

Brock Yates (1991) sums up the Ferrari 'palace revolution', which Phil Hill learned about almost immediately after signing for 1962, as a combination of complex factors, none of which entirely explains what happened; and as all the participants had such vested interests at stake, it was unlikely the true course of events would ever become clear, though many spoke about it later. Although there had been little or no 'outside' knowledge of a Ferrari rift, after the fact many commentators settled for Signora Laura Ferrari's 'meddling' in company and team affairs as the primary reason for the defection of at least eight important Ferrari company directors. Yates argues that while Signora Ferrari may have been involved, the more significant issues were Enzo Ferrari's jealousy over control of his growing company. He had never been comfortable with outspoken men in his team, whether they were engineers or drivers, and Chiti and Tavoni were strong people with a loyal following. Yates summarises the conflict as having been triggered by Laura Ferrari's behaviour but essentially saw it as 'Ferrari's decision to centralize and consolidate power within his rapidly growing operation' (Yates, 1992, p. 342).

Fuelled by a series of internal memoranda (published later as a book ostensibly by Ferrari himself but in reality the result of a number of conversations with journalist Gianni Roghi), there was considerable bluffing and counter-bluffing between Ferrari and Chiti (planning and race management), Tavoni (sporting management), Ermanno Della Casa (administrative management), Federico Gilberti (production and supply management), Giotto Bizzarrini (control and testing management, the designer who had brought Chiti to Maranello), Geralamo Gardini (commercial management), Fausto Galazzi (foundry and metallurgical management) and Enzo Selmi (personnel management). In the end, this group was out-bluffed by Ferrari and all 'resigned'. Some eventually returned, while others were considered traitors by Ferrari.

Enzo had sent Laura Ferrari as his representative to von Trips's funeral, accompanied by Amerigo Manicardi, who was responsible for Ferrari sales worldwide. It rained. The coffin was carried on the back of von Trips's 250 Spyder behind an old woman carrying a lamp, but the clutch was burnt out before they got to the cemetery. To make an already difficult situation worse, Laura Ferrari tried to get a ride back to Modena with Phil Hill and Richie Ginther, because she didn't like Manicardi – the feelings were apparently mutual. According to Hill, he and Richie told her they were going to Sweden, which wasn't true; they were nearly caught out as Manicardi's car passed them on the return journey and Signora Ferrari asked if that wasn't Hill's Peugeot. Hill said Manicardi was a very pleasant man, but when he died of a heart attack at an early age, Ferrari sent no one to his funeral. This had taken place in September when resentment over Laura Ferrari's 'meddling' was beginning to peak.

Ferrari officially announced the resignations in the last week of November, though the individuals concerned had departed earlier and tensions had been building up since von Trips's funeral. Tavoni and Chiti had been told not to go to the funeral by Enzo Ferrari lest they get caught off-guard and say things that might harm the beleaguered team. They refused to obey, but didn't understand Ferrari's motives at the time. Shortly after this, in a meeting in Ferrari's office where Laura Ferrari insisted that she be a part of decisions affecting the company, Gardini argued against her, and got slapped by her for his troubles. Later the same day in a restaurant in Modena, Gardini and Ferrari exchanged some sharp words about the matter in front of Luigi Chinetti, and Ferrari used this event to focus the 'blame' on Gardini. Gardini's colleagues all worked to support him, but by this time Ferrari seemed certain that it was in his best interest either to beat the opposition down or be done with them, and the resignations were forced. Two Italian journalists, Oscar Orefici and Piero Casucci, had the respect and attention of Carlo Chiti, and over many years he unravelled for them the complex details of his final days at Ferrari and his move to form ATS (Orefici, 1991; Casucci, 1987). Chiti, however, did express the feeling that leaving wasn't the wisest decision; he rather wished he hadn't shut the door or had the door shut on him by Ferrari.

Tavoni, who remained silent and refused to discuss the matter for many years, was somewhat more open with Graham Gauld in 1998, pointing the finger more firmly at Laura Ferrari and Enzo's willingness to allow her to interfere in the company activities. Tavoni was of the opinion that Laura had a strong influence over her husband, and that it was easier for him to let others deal with her. She had attended a number of races since the late 1950s, but occasionally her behaviour bordered on the bizarre, and she slapped Tavoni in public on at least one occasion. Tavoni argues it was the other directors' wish to complain about her in writing to Ferrari that brought the internal tensions to a head. In reality, he admitted, they did not resign but were fired.

All of this meant that suddenly Mauro Forghieri, who had been one of Ferrari's quiet men and had essentially been playing a secondary role to Chiti, was in charge of technical matters. At the age of twenty-six he effectively replaced Chiti. Forghieri has always remained reluctant to discuss the events of late 1961, and in an interview with Guy Mangiamele for *Cavallino* (No. 49, February/March, 1989, p. 18) he played down his role in, and his understanding of, what was happening among the people he had been working with for the previous year and a half: '. . . at any rate, for some reason which I don't know, at this time there was a political problem between the management of the Factory and the boss. Chiti, della Casa, Gilberti, and others, and all of the management, left the Factory. About the end of 1961, I think. So, the only engineer left at the Factory was me.'

Around the same time, rumours suggested that Hill and Ginther were to be asked to accept a pay cut for 1962 to save on costs. Ginther had been retained as a part-timer and his contract specified that he would do testing and remain on call for a number of tasks but he didn't have a clear role in the team, in spite of his brilliant race performances.

Brock Yates recounts the meeting between Ginther and Enzo Ferrari. It was described to him by Ginther:

The meeting took place in Ferrari's Maranello office, a dingy, stark, blue-walled room that had taken on the trappings of a shrine. It was virtually empty, having only a small conference table and a large photograph of the smiling Dino facing the ingegnere's immense, totally bare desk. Beneath the portrait of his dead son was a vase filled with fresh flowers. These were strange, somewhat sinister surroundings in which Ferrari enjoyed a powerful psychological advantage. He handed Ginther a contract. It was more or less the same as the one he had offered the year before. Ginther scanned it, then refused to sign it. 'Sign it or you'll never drive in Formula One again,' said Ferrari darkly. Ginther wadded up the paper and tossed it in Ferrari's lap. Ferrari said nothing, then buzzed for one of his assistants. 'Take the key to Signor Ginther's car and check in the trunk to be sure the jack is still there,' he said imperiously. And so ended, rather inelegantly, Richie Ginther's short but illustrious career in Maranello. (Yates, 1992, p. 344)

Ginther went off to spend three years at BRM, where he had a number of fine races, and at the Bourne headquarters he was respected for his testing talent, but he didn't win a Grand Prix until 1965, when, ironically, he took the last race of the 1.5-litre formula in Mexico for Honda.

In mid-autumn, John Surtees had an offer to visit Ferrari to discuss driving for them in 1962. He told the author:

I had this offer to drive for them, as I had the year before, but I didn't feel ready for it then, and I still didn't think I was right for them so I turned them down a second time. I didn't want to go off and get involved in the politics then, but when I decided to go in 1963, it seemed a better time. They were down by then and I felt better in an Italian team when they were down. This had also given me a chance to think about other things such as driving sports cars which were looking good by then. I also felt I could deal with the politics, but, yes, I had had offers from Ferrari for 1962.

Potentially a most interesting development, and one that could have had a major impact on the 1962 season, was the series of contacts made between Enzo Ferrari, Stirling Moss, Moss's father Alfred and Ken Gregory – the last two were running the UDT-Laystall Team which had been BRP. While discussions were going on about the possibility of Moss driving a Rob Walker-run 'sharknose', a plan was hatched for UDT-Laystall to run a Ferrari GTO in GT events and one of the rear-engined sports cars, most likely the 246SP, which the team would loan out when Moss was unavailable. Rob Walker talked to the author about the plans:

This was entirely set up by Stirling and Ken Gregory, but Stirling told me all about it, though how he organised it with Ferrari I am not certain. Ferrari had a very high regard for Stirling and he actually built the car and painted it in our colours. Then Stirling had his accident so Innes Ireland drove it here at Silverstone in the International Trophy. It was going to run in dark blue and white. It started back in 1960 when Stirling had his accident at Spa. I had a contract with BP to run at all Grand Prix races for them. I think they paid me £10,000 and they paid Stirling £10,000 and that was good money in those days. I felt I had an obligation to BP because Stirling was out of racing, and I thought of two points: that it would be good to run a Ferrari 250 GT in the Tourist Trophy as it would fill up the races Stirling wasn't doing, and then it would be good for Stirling to practise in an ordinary car before he got back into a Formula 1 car. Of course, he won so easily, we thought we would do it again. Then we ran it through the season. We never had to do anything to it and it won every race that it ran in. I didn't like it very much but he loved it. It used to have a terrific tramp when you accelerated. Stirling probably just drove through the tramp and he thought it was great. One of the funny things about Stirling was that he was so loyal. He would be driving for Vanwall, and then the next race he'd be driving for me. When he was driving for Vanwall he virtually wouldn't talk to me and when he was driving for me he wouldn't talk to Vanwall. He would just cut it off absolutely.

Moss spoke with his usual frankness about how he nearly became a Ferrari Grand Prix driver and his relationship with Enzo Ferrari:

Ferrari had invited me to drive for him at Bari in 1951 and when I showed up, the car had been assigned to Taruffi. That made me decide 'Sod him. If he's going to mess me around, I'm not going to drive for him anymore.' I did drive a Ferrari on thirteen occasions. I was

Above: Rodriguez and Bandini await the start of the Pau Grand Prix on 23 April 1962. They finished second and fifth. (Graeme Simpson/Motor Racing Tradition) *Below*: Rodriguez on the twisty Pau street circuit, 1962. (Graeme Simpson)

Above: Innes Ireland driving chassis 0001 at the Silverstone International Trophy. The car was loaned to him by Ferrari as a mark of respect for Stirling Moss, who had been injured at Goodwood a few weeks earlier. (Author's Collection) *Below*: Baghetti drives chassis 0007 at the Dutch Grand Prix, 1962. (Archive von Trips/Fodisch)

Rodriguez in the Hunzerug behind the pits at Zandvoort, 1962. (Archive von Trips/Fodisch)

Above: Hill (36) and Bandini (38) are ninth and tenth on the grid with Surtees (28), Salvadori (26) and Ginther (8) behind, Monaco, 1962. (Archive von Trips/Fodisch) *Below*: Willy Mairesse on lap 1, Monaco, 1962. (Graeme Simpson/Motor Racing Tradition)

Above: The Ferrari transporter arrives at Spa, 1962. (Brian Joscelyne) *Below*: The Ferrari garage prior to practice at the Belgian Grand Prix, Spa, 1962. (Brian Joscelyne)

Cars line up in the downhill pit lane, Spa, 1962. (Brian Joscelyne)

Hill's chassis 0009 before practice, Spa, 1962. (Brian Joscelyne)

Baghetti's car, chassis 0001, Belgian Grand Prix, Spa, 1962. (Brian Joscelyne)

Bandini arrives to join the team at Spa in 1962, though he wasn't driving. (Brian Joscelyne)

Willy Mairesse at La Source hairpin during practice for the Belgian Grand Prix, 1962. (Brian Joscelyne)

The battle between Hill and Rodriguez, Spa, 1962. (Brian Joscelyne)

Phil Hill exits La Source in practice, Spa, 1962. (Graeme Simpson/Motor Racing Tradition)

Mairesse is behind Taylor on this lap as they leave La Source, Spa, 1962. (Brian Joscelyne)

Above: German photographer Jerry Sloniger took this ghostly multiple exposure of Bandini being pursued by Rodriguez at Monza in 1962. (Jerry Sloniger) *Below*: Rock musician Chris Rea in his 'sharknose' reproduction. (Raymond Jenkins)

disqualified once at Sebring and the fan blade came off at Le Mans, but the other eleven times I won, so I have good memories of Ferrari. Then in the end of 1961 I went to see him in Modena. He actually built the car for me and sent it over, and Innes drove it. The deal was that I would drive for him, provided Rob Walker ran it. I said, 'You can look after it and Rob will run it' and he had agreed to this, which was quite a big step forward. I remember going down there and arriving. People say you wait outside for ages, but as soon as I arrived I was shown straight in and he said 'Tell me what car you want', talking about the sports car. We talked about what I was going to do and he said, 'You tell me what car you want and I'll build it for you. Do you want four cylinders, six cylinders, eight?' I said, 'I think the 246 is probably the one', and he said, 'We'll do that.' I said, 'Are you happy that Rob runs the F1 car?', and he was happy with that, and then he showed me around and we shook hands and went off to get something to eat across the road. I had gone down there because the Ferrari wasn't doing as well as I thought it might. I normally stick with English cars but I thought maybe it was time to try something different so I went down to see him. He had spoken to me and I knew the door was open. Rob was going to run the car and Ferrari was going to maintain it. I suppose that meant it would go back to them after one or two races. Alf Francis would look after it and he would be my pit crew and we would enter it as a Rob Walker entry. I would also have the sports car which BRP would run.

The author asked Moss to speculate on what might have happened had he not had his Goodwood accident in April 1962 and had therefore driven and developed the car. Did he think he and it had world championship potential?

I thought it had the potential, and we would have been running in parallel with Ferrari so I think it would have worked for all of us. One thing you must remember, when Ferrari asked me to drive I went and asked Fangio what he thought. He said, 'Drive for him but don't sign for him', which I thought was an interesting input. The great thing about Ferrari was that you can't tell me of any Ferrari that has had a wheel fall off or where things break and the car hurts you, and I thought that security would be something nice. I have a great respect for Ferrari and everything he did for motor racing. He was an amazing person, even though I didn't agree with his ethics. I had seen the car and had raced against it and I knew its strengths and weaknesses. At Monaco in 1961 I could see where I had a nicer car, no doubt about it. It was much more user friendly but it didn't have the power. As the year went on they seemed to have improved the handling, but I knew the strength of the Ferrari and if I could have gone into the following year as expected, I was convinced that I could have a more winning package than I had. Cooper wasn't giving us any help and they wouldn't sell us a gearbox, and Lotus wouldn't give me the latest car either. They would only sell us the one from the year before. It seemed an intelligent

Moss and Fangio in 1963 after Moss had recovered from his Goodwood accident. (Jim Gleave/Atlantic Art)

decision to make, though I hadn't even had a ride in one of the Ferrari 'sharknose' cars.

While all this deliberation and planning was going on, three non-championship races were run. The first was at Zeltweg in Austria on 17 September; Ireland took it in the Lotus from Brabham. Then Moss won the Gold Cup at Oulton Park in England on 23 September, taking the four-wheel drive Ferguson to a win in the wet, and on 1 October Tony Marsh won an essentially British privateers' race at Brands Hatch. The final Grand Prix of the year was the US event at Watkins Glen. Innes Ireland scored a notable victory for Team Lotus ahead of Dan Gurney and Tony Brooks. The author attended this race, his first ever Grand Prix.

FIVE

1962
WHAT GOES UP . . .

In his review of the 1961 season, *Motorsport*'s Formula 1 correspondent Denis Jenkinson was effusive in his praise of the new formula. He admitted to surprise at how successful the new regulations had been: not only had many previous lap times been matched, but they had been bettered on some circuits, and most average race speeds had increased. There had been the spectacle of very considerable close racing, with very few processions all season long. Jenkinson wasn't the only one to feel that the rule changes had been vindicated and that some great racing had been the result, though there remained a lingering feeling that a reduction in engine size wasn't a guarantee of either safer or better racing, and the return to bigger displacement engines was still anticipated.

At Ferrari, the new season was approaching, and outsiders could have been forgiven for thinking the team was in turmoil after the departure of so many key staff. But that would be to underestimate the number of good engineers and consultants Enzo Ferrari always kept close to him. Expertise in depth was always a Ferrari hallmark, though his choice of some staff was not easily understandable. If 1961 had been the year of Chiti, was 1962 going to be Forghieri's? The answer, briefly, is no, but that is not to discredit Mauro Forghieri at all. First, much of what Chiti had developed in 1961 was intended for long-term use, and Forghieri had a hand in a number of these developments, so there were still aspects of the improvement to follow up on. Forghieri has always tended to see the 156, particularly in 1961 and 1962, as the car on which he learned about chassis development, and he believes that his real and long-lasting contributions came later, especially when the 3-litre formula arrived. In some senses, 1962 was the year of Dragoni who had been brought in to replace Tavoni, essentially as team manager. Dragoni was an example of how ego could rule at Ferrari, and it wasn't long before his influence was felt within the team – generally not to its benefit. The battle of the egos continued, and in some ways this did not help Forghieri play a more positive role during 1962. While Chiti himself was a person of big ego, he tended not to use this to the detriment of the drivers and the rest of the team: Dragoni did, often making Forghieri's job more difficult. Some accounts also argue that 'Phil Hill simply didn't hit it off with the new

The F1 car at the 1962 Ferrari press day. (BRSCC Archive)

designer' (Henry, 1997, p. 93), but Phil himself would not be drawn on this, settling for the view that the battle of the egos caused a number of difficulties and that he didn't particularly 'get along' with engineer Forghieri.

When 24 February, the traditional Ferrari press day, came around, there were a number of changes evident in the car for the coming season. How far Chiti's planning for 1962 had progressed before his exit is difficult to judge from his own writings and interviews and from what has been said by others. Clearly, two major areas of development had been started – one in relation to the cylinder heads and the other concerning the gearbox – and some of this work had been going on earlier in 1961. Ferrari had pressed Forghieri and his young design engineer colleague Angelo Bellei to each design a 1.5-litre engine, though in the end neither was used for 1962. Chiti's engine development colleagues Walter Salvarani and Franco Rocchi continued work on the 120-degree unit because Chiti had been considering several alternative cylinder head designs including two valves per cylinder with twin plugs, two valves with three plugs, three valves with two plugs and four valves per cylinder with a single plug. Long-time consultants Vittorio Jano and Luigi Bazzi remained on hand to assist in these development tasks, so the loss of Chiti and co. might not have seemed so great. Nevertheless, one would have to be very optimistic to believe that such changes of personnel could take place without a serious loss of performance.

When the cars were uncovered for the press, they had the prototype heads with four valves per cylinder and a single central spark plug, and the shape of the rear bodywork indicated the existence of the new six-speed gearbox which was now located between the engine and the final drive rather than behind the differential. The exposed clutch remained at the rear of the assembly. Baghetti had been out testing the six-speed gearbox at Modena in mid-December. It was alleged that Phil Hill had used a six-speed gearbox at Monza, but this was evidently not announced at the time. Hill had indeed had gearbox maladies in practice at Monza.

Ferrari announced that the car would race in this form, and considerable fuss was made of the new heads. The 120-degree engine was said to be producing 200bhp at 10,000rpm, and this meant the usable peak engine speed had been increased by 1000rpm. The 1961 engine problems had been mainly due to valve gear failure and spring breakages. The lighter reciprocating weights and smaller lifts which are associated with four valves per cylinder layouts were an answer to the old problem of the loads that occur in the Jano-type arrangement; in this design, the cams operate directly on a collar threaded on to the valve stems and the latter absorb the side thrust of the cam and the cam layout

Opposite: The relatively simple multi-tube structure of the 'sharknose' is clear in this 1962 chassis on show at the press day. (John Godfrey Collection)

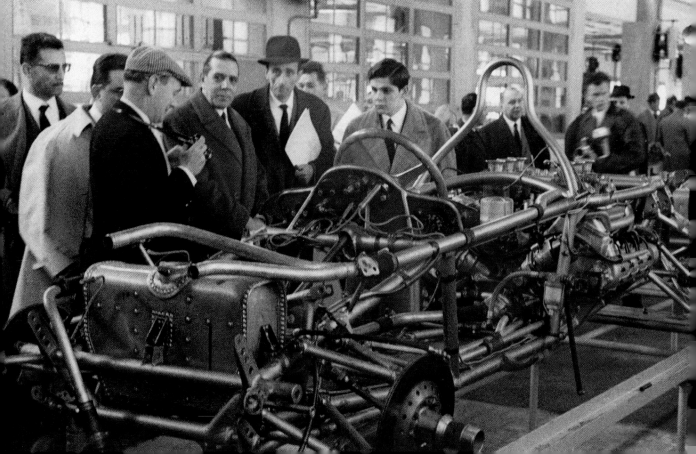

also subjects the springs to bending and relatively heavy torsional loads. Ferrari wasn't the only team considering four valves per cylinder, but the irony is that in the event the cars appeared at the races in 1962 with the same format as in 1961, and even the 65-degree engine was being used with some experimental changes. This seemed indicative of what Ferrari had really lost with Chiti's departure.

The engines had the same layout of triple-choke Weber carburettors per bank as in 1961, and although the twin ports on the heads merged into a single entry at the carb joint, this did not match what was thought to be required for a four valves per cylinder arrangement, that is, a six choke per bank arrangement. This design was retained: presumably because either Ferrari had no intention of using the four-valve layout, or never got it sorted in time.

The rearrangement of the transmission layout was something of a puzzle to those inspecting the new car, especially because Enzo Ferrari went out of his way to say the cars were essentially the same as in 1961. Moving the mass forward was presumed to reduce further oversteer characteristics and induce some understeer, though Phil Hill had been saying since the first tests in 1960 that he 'couldn't understand why they were always stuck with so much negative camber', and limited attention seemed to have been given to this flaw. Some work had been done on the issue of roll steer and a tubular wishbone was now installed, but with the upper and lower pivots mounted on ball joints A third transverse locating member also appeared at hub level mounted on ball pivots, giving a small degree of rear steering when the wheels were deflected from their normal static position (Mundy, *Autocar*, 4 May 1962).

Slight modifications to the chassis had been incorporated and the wheelbase had been lengthened just under 2 inches to 9½; this produced at least the appearance of a slightly shorter rear section. Weight was up by some 100lbs, though this was later reduced by some 65lbs and both front and rear track was increased by some 5ins. There is some evidence that the track was changed on more than one occasion, and after Ireland drove it in early May at the International Trophy, recommendations were made to increase it even further, but Phil Hill felt this was not an improvement. Visible differences seen at the February press day also included a windscreen with a slightly increased rake and 'bulged fairings behind the cool air intakes on each side of the engine bay' (Nye, 1979, p. 137).

Alan Brinton, reporting the press day in *Motor Racing* (April 1962), emphasised Ferrari's plan that six new F1 machines would be built, two for each driver. Three would have a seriously modified 120-degree engine and three would have the 65-degree unit. The 120-degree cars were to be run at the faster circuits, and the 65-degree cars at the slower courses.

The team also announced the driver line-up at the press day, and in typical Ferrari fashion there was a degree of confusion about it. Phil Hill was clearly the senior member, though his pay may not have reflected this, and some accounts say the other regulars were Baghetti, Ricardo Rodriguez and Lorenzo Bandini, with Willy Mairesse taking over Ginther's role as chief test driver and Olivier Gendebien reserved on the F1 books

Opposite, above: Lorenzo Bandini examines the modified chassis with its 65-degree engine in place. (Ferret Fotographic)

Below: This chassis has the new four valves per cylinder engine in place but the engine was never used during the 1962 season. (Ferret Fotographic)

The 1962 chassis, which varied very little from the 1961 version. (Ferret Fotographic)

Journalist Bernard Cahier, to the left of the car, discusses the new machine, press day, 1962. (Ferret Fotographic)

Drivers for 1962: Giancarlo Baghetti (left), Willy Mairesse and Lorenzo Bandini (far right) with Ferrari mechanics at the press day. (Ferret Fotographic)

A 1962 car with the 120-degree engine. Severe negative camber is still obvious on the rear suspension. (Ferret Fotographic)

too. Who had what kind of contract is a matter for conjecture, and according to Nye (1979), Rodriguez was more of a part-timer like Gendebien and was also seen as a strong member of the sports car line-up that would include brother Pedro.

Bandini had been brought in at the urging of the new team manager Eugenio Dragoni, who had been influential in getting Baghetti into the team. The Milanese Bandini was a pleasant, non-political and friendly person who had got his start in the Mille Miglia rally, where he won his class in 1958. He drove front-engined Formula Junior Volpini and Stanguellini cars in 1959, before having his first taste of F1 in 1960 with Centro Sud's Cooper-Maserati, which he drove competently if not brilliantly through that year and into 1961. He was also a competent performer in the races he drove in 1962 but was dropped from the team for early 1963, coming back later in the year and remaining until his tragic death in a Ferrari at Monaco in 1967. He was often a pawn in Dragoni's battle for power, especially when John Surtees was in the Ferrari line-up.

As has perhaps become clear, the official appearance of the 53-year-old Eugenio Dragoni on the scene at the beginning of 1962 – he had been close to Ferrari unofficially for some time – was not welcomed by many. He had been involved in a Milan pharmaceutical business, had been a director of the Milan-based Scuderia Sant Ambroeus, and had had a close association with motor racing for some years. He was the antithesis of the generally easy-going and flexible Tavoni whom he replaced and has been described as 'imperious, opinionated and uncommunicative . . . and devious' (Godfrey, 1993, p. 23). He had an overbearing manner, but was a good organiser and a strict, somewhat autocratic, disciplinarian. He came to be known for the destructive way in which he attempted to play one driver off against another. Phil Hill became his particular target, and, according to Godfrey (1993, p. 23), 'he never missed an opportunity to undermine Hill's standing in the team and with Enzo Ferrari'. Dragoni saw Bandini as 'his' future champion and set out to promote him, regardless of either his performance or that of other drivers in the team. He was ultimately the reason for Surtees' leaving Ferrari in 1966. Whereas Tavoni might have been criticised for not being tough enough and occasionally faltering in the face of difficult decisions, Dragoni was virtually the opposite. Ferrari's announcement of Dragoni's appointment was worded in such a way as to indicate that Laura Ferrari would have little influence on the team in 1962.

During the winter of 1961/2 a number of stories had circulated about what would happen in the 1962 season. *Autosport* carried the announcement that Ferrari would have V8 and V12 engines in F1, and that Jano would be replacing Chiti. There was also word of the new all-Maserati F1 car with a V12, the continuation of the Inter-Continental series and the retirement of Tony Brooks. Scuderia Centro Sud, under Guglielmo 'Mimmo' Dei, announced it was being disbanded and that this would free Bandini to drive for Ferrari, although his original contract with Centro Sud was for all of 1962. The Centro Sud closure was also partly linked to Dei's anger over Baghetti having been named Italian champion in 1961 instead of Bandini, who seemed to have more of a claim on the title. *Autosport* (9 March 1962) carried a report from the Italian newspaper *Gazzetta dello Sport* that Ferrari was constructing an air-cooled eight-cylinder in-line engine, with the engine and gearbox mounted, transversely, between the driver and rear wheels. The car was expected to make its debut at Monza in September.

There was continuous comment during the winter of 1961/2 about the departure of 'the eight' from Ferrari, and indeed there had been a number of interviews with Enzo, including one by a certain Bernard Ronald of *Motor Racing* magazine. Now Ronald never appeared on the masthead of that magazine, so the author suspects this was one of the several pseudonyms the publication used at the time. In retrospect, and perhaps because we live in a much more cynical age nowadays, it is surprising that Enzo Ferrari almost always seemed to be taken at his word by journalists. Ronald describes the post-'palace revolution' atmosphere in these terms: 'Obviously Ferrari, a noble man of ideals and generous to a fault, has been hurt to the quick by the swiftness of events, and the almost equally swift reaction of zealous journalists from far and wide.' (*Motor Racing*, January, 1962, p. 13). Earlier in the article Ronald apologised for upsetting Ferrari by asking him what had happened. There are also very few instances of anyone asking the Commendatore why he hadn't delivered what he had promised some months before. This just wasn't done: Ronald had asked but didn't get an answer.

In addition to changes going on inside the teams and rumours of technical developments, there were nine major races scheduled before the European non-championship race at Brussels on 1 April. Trevor Taylor scored his maiden F1 victory in his Lotus at the Cape Grand Prix in Killarney, South Africa, ahead of Jim Clark. In the long series of 'down under' races to Inter-Continental/Formula Libre rules, Moss won the opening New Zealand Grand Prix at Ardmore in the 2.5-litre Lotus-Climax with Surtees second, and Brabham took the next round in Wellington in his 2.7 Cooper-Climax, with Moss second. The results were reversed for the following race – the Lady Wigram Trophy – and McLaren beat them both to take the Teretonga Trophy at Invercargill. This race took place during the same week in which UDT-Laystall ordered three Climax V8 and two BRM V8 engines for their Lotus team to be run for Moss, Gregory and Ireland. The racing circus then moved to Australia for four rounds, the first at Warwick Farm going to Moss who was again ahead of McLaren. Then Brabham beat Bib Stillwell at the Lakeside GP near Brisbane. Surtees beat Brabham at Longford, Tasmania, but the result went the other way for the final round at Sandown Park, with Brabham again in front.

Back in February, Phil Hill and Ricardo Rodriguez had led the Daytona 3-Hours, the opening round of the Championship for Manufacturers, in their Ferrari Dino 246SP, but Dan Gurney eventually got past after a lengthy fuel stop by the NART mechanics to provide a rare win for a Lotus 19B in a major sports car race. At Sebring for the 12-Hours on 23 March, Hill was again second, this time with Gendebien in the NART 250GTO, while Bonnier and Lucien Bianchi won in the Scuderia Venezia 250TR/61.

The expected season opener at Siracusa, where Baghetti had his remarkable win in 1961, had been cancelled so the first significant Formula 1 race for 1962 was the Grand Prix of Brussels. The race was run over three 22-lap heats of the 4.5 kilometre street circuit in Heysel, on the outskirts of Brussels, very close to the Atomium. Heysel, a damp Belgian kerb-lined set of public roads, was to be the first test of Ferrari race-worthiness. Belgian driver Willy Mairesse had managed to persuade Ferrari to send a car for him. This was chassis 0006, which Denis Jenkinson mistakenly called a 'new car' – in fact it was the chassis raced at Monza by Ricardo Rodriguez. Nye (1979) also got it wrong when he said the car had a 120-degree engine. There were many 'new' aspects to the car, but the engine was a 65-degree unit, although it had had a fair amount of experimental work done on it. There was no sign of the four valves per cylinder, but the bore and stroke had been modified to 67×70mm giving a capacity of 1480.73cc and producing a claimed 185–190bhp. The car had the six-speed gearbox with 1961 front suspension, but the rear suspension had been altered and thus became known as the '1962 suspension'. This included the transverse strut seen at the press day. There was a new oil tank fitted in the nose of the car with air cooling tubes passing through it. The 18-volt electrical system had been maintained. Perspex air scoops were added at the rear for cooling the Dunlop inboard rear brakes, and the exhaust pipes were shorter than on the previous year's car.

Willy Mairesse leads Stirling Moss on his way to winning the non-championship Brussels Grand Prix at the Heysel street circuit, 1962. (Author's Collection)

Heavy rain in the first practice on Friday precluded any fast times, but there was a sign of things to come when Tony Marsh started running very quickly in horrible conditions in the new, slimmer BRM V8. Marsh had been loaned the second car because Ginther had been slightly injured in testing and had sustained some burns. Graham Hill in the number one BRM was finding it difficult to get used to the speed with which the engine came on the cam, while Stirling Moss, in the Lotus that had been his Monza practice car, was going as quickly as usual in the wet. The Rob Walker Lotus 18 in which Moss had won the German Grand Prix had been sold to Scuderia Venezia, but Nino Vaccarella damaged it severely when he went off in Saturday's slightly drier practice before he could set a good qualifying time.

Mairesse went fifth fastest as the road dried out late on Saturday, but not before he missed a gear and came into the pits with the needle stuck on 12000rpm. The gauge only goes that far and the Ferrari mechanic just dropped a rag over it. Both BRMs had also been to the dizzy heights of 12000rpm and survived. None of the three engines were changed for the race.

Jim Clark had squeezed his Lotus 24-Climax on to pole position, but was beaten off the line in heat one by Moss, who rushed down the hill from the start, under the autoroute then around through the houses built right on the edge of the road, but he then promptly locked up and slid down the escape road. Though Moss made a superb comeback to second at the end of the heat, Graham Hill won from Mairesse, who drove steadily and with unaccustomed control. Clark had broken valve gear.

The second heat started after four in the afternoon in the order of finish in the first heat, and results were to be based on finishing order rather than time. The two BRMs wouldn't move and were push-started, for which they were then disqualified, as Moss drove away into the lead on lap 3 from Mairesse and John Surtees in the new Lola. Mairesse was desperate to hang on to Moss and spun wildly on the sixth tour. Mairesse then reversed back out on to the circuit, against the rules, striking Trevor Taylor's wheel which fell off as the Ferrari sped away. Moss then had valve failure and Mairesse, now driving exceptionally well, moved from fifth back into the lead and kept it. To the surprise of the non-Belgians, he was not penalised for his traffic manoeuvre.

Only ten cars came to the line for heat three. 'Wild Willy' went into the lead on the second lap and stayed there, and there were virtually no changes of position during the whole twenty-two laps. Bonnier was second and Ireland third. This had been a promising start to the year, because Mairesse, like Baghetti in 1961, won the opening race in which the 'sharknose' had been entered. When the cars were weighed, the Ferrari came in at 1199lbs, somewhat more than had been announced in February.

Jim Clark won the Lombank Trophy for F1 cars from Hill's BRM and Bonnier's four-cylinder Porsche at Snetterton on 14 April. Then on Easter Monday, the Glover Trophy race at Goodwood saw Stirling Moss out in the UDT-Laystall Lotus 24. Moss was chasing Graham Hill on the thirty-fifth lap when he suddenly went straight into the St Mary's Bank, suffering injuries that kept him in hospital for months, ended his career and changed the face of contemporary motor racing. His success rate at the time had been so great that he remained one of the strong contenders for the championship in 1962.

Ferrari was to take part in four more F1 races before the first championship Grand Prix in Holland on 20 May. The first of these was at the tiny and twisty street circuit at Pau in the French Pyrenees on 23 April, the scene of some outstanding road races in the past. Ferrari, with Dragoni now firmly in charge, sent two cars: 0006, the Brussels car with the 65-degree engine, for Lorenzo Bandini to make his Ferrari Formula 1 debut, and chassis 0003 with the 120-degree engine for Ricardo Rodriguez. The cars were very similar, being referred to as 'interim' 1962 machines which meant they both had the updated rear suspension and six-speed gearbox behind the axle, not in front of it. The Rodriguez car was the one Baghetti had driven at Monza.

Team Lotus and Jack Brabham had decided to miss Goodwood to come to Pau. Rob Walker had sent his Lotus 24-Climax so UDT-Laystall could run it for Moss, while Walker borrowed the UDT Lotus-Climax four-cylinder car for Maurice Trintignant, something of a veteran here. Jim Clark was fastest in both the Saturday and Sunday practice sessions for the 100-lap race, which was to be run on the Monday. Pau consists of fourteen tight corners and almost no straight and seemed to favour the better-handling new Lotus. However, it was Trintignant in the old 1960 Lotus who surprised everyone on the first day. Trintignant had raced here before but had never been in a Lotus, while Bandini had done well at Pau the previous year but so far hadn't sampled the Ferrari. Rodriguez, on the other hand, knew his car but had never been to Pau. Although Clark got pole, Rodriguez was there in the middle of the front row with Bonnier third. Brabham and Trintignant were next, and Bandini was down in sixth spot.

Clark in the Lotus had fully expected Rodriguez to attempt a quick start in order to build up a lead on a circuit where overtaking is very difficult, but the first three remained fairly close for nine laps, with Rodriguez just holding off Clark. The author spoke with Trintignant about Pau at the Monaco Historics in May 2000:

Rodriguez on the way to his best F1 result in his short career, Pau, 1962. (Ferrari Centro Documentazione)

Well, I think it was my first race that year and I hadn't driven the Lotus before but it was a very nice car to drive, and right for that circuit. I remember that I got past the Porsche, Bonnier I think, and went after Ricardo. He was smooth, which I thought was good because I didn't think the Ferrari was very good for that type circuit, but he was quick. I was very comfortable and I managed to get past him after a few laps and went after Clark. He then had a gearbox problem, and so did I later, but then it seemed to be all right and I managed to stay in front to the end. It wasn't bad for my age. What was I? Forty-four. So it was a good race and I was a little surprised to win but I thought I had driven well.

And indeed he had: he finished 45 seconds in front of a cautious Rodriguez. Jack Lewis, who was all over Rodriguez in the tight corners, just couldn't get past but had another good race, finishing third; Bandini could only manage fifth. Ferrari now had a first, a second and a fifth in the bag, so the season was still looking good as the team headed for the Aintree 200 only a few days later.

Conditions were dry for once at Aintree as the cars arrived for practice on Friday 26 April. Ferrari sent two cars, one for Phil Hill and one for Giancarlo Baghetti. Baghetti had chassis 0001, last seen in Ginther's hands at the Nürburgring the previous August; it had its 120-degree engine and six-speed gearbox but with the gearbox mounted behind the final drive. Hill had 0007, which hadn't been used before but appeared to be the basic 1961 chassis with 1962's modifications incorporated. It also had the 120-degree engine but there was no sign of the four valves per cylinder, the usual two valves being employed as before. Hill had the six-speed box but this was mounted ahead of the final drive for the first time.

The Aintree 200 was notable for two things. Jim Clark established himself very clearly as a, or possibly *the*, top-line driver now that Moss was absent. He had been coming along steadily in 1961 but was now showing more than the occasional flash of brilliance. He put pole position out of reach of the others at Aintree by setting a 1 minute 53.8 seconds lap, 4 seconds quicker than the previous 1.5-litre record set by Brooks in 1961 and 3 seconds ahead of the outright circuit record. The other notable occurrence was that the Ferraris struggled to get below 2 minutes, though Hill did 1 minute 57.4 seconds in the second session to Baghetti's 1 minute 57.6 seconds. They were 3½ seconds off pole and it was clear that the 1962 Ferrari was in trouble. Apparently Baghetti had used 12000rpm at one point, and Hill was pretty close on 11000. It is true that Hill was down with the flu and Baghetti hadn't driven at Aintree in the dry, but Hill was unhappy about the car's handling. He spoke to the author about the machine he found himself driving at Aintree:

I ended up with a car that was not what it had pretended to be before I even signed up and that is, it was going to be a quicker car than my 1961 car. I ended up with the car that had the gearbox in the middle instead of at the rear and they had my car some 45mm wider. As soon

Opposite, above: Phil Hill drove to third at an uncharacteristically dry Aintree 200 in 1962. (Raymond Jenkins)

Below: Hill in chassis 0007. (Ferret Fotographic)

Baghetti at Aintree in chassis
0001. (Ferret Fotographic)

as we got to the faster circuits, my car wouldn't pull last year's gears. I wouldn't say my car was worse, because it was the better car on short, twisty circuits and also it was easier to drive, but lots of times an easier car to drive doesn't mean anything at all.

The two Ferraris circulated in sixth and seventh place for much of the race with Clark way out in front. Baghetti had a successful scrap with Gregory and Ireland. Hill felt ill and his condition was made worse by fumes in the cockpit, but he drove well and passed Surtees. Graham Hill's retirement saw Phil move up to third behind Clark and Bruce McLaren, but Baghetti closed to within a second of Hill at the end. This had clearly not been a good race for Ferrari. In fact it was the worst performance for some time despite the final placing. It was at Aintree that Dragoni's innuendos about Hill's commitment seemed to have started.

Ferrari's participation in the International Trophy meeting at Silverstone on 12 May was unusual. Enzo Ferrari had asked to see UDT-Laystall team manager Ken Gregory at Maranello on the Wednesday after Aintree. Colonel Ronnie Hoare of Maranello Concessionaires and Innes Ireland accompanied Gregory. Ferrari, who seemed genuinely upset over Moss's accident and his consequent inability to drive in a Ferrari for the rest of the season, offered to lend Baghetti's Aintree car, chassis 0001, to UDT for Ireland to drive. The car arrived at Maranello Concessionaires in England with a pale green stripe painted on it, this being Ferrari's own gesture. Ireland qualified the car sixth for the 52-lap race, but was nearly 3 seconds slower than Graham Hill's pole time.

The story of that race is best told in Innes Ireland's own words:

> The 'shark-nosed' 156 F1 Ferrari duly turned up for practice in a large transporter with a team of mechanics and six technicians which impressed me no end. Since I had been asked by the Commendatore to make a report on every aspect of the car I was particularly careful not to be hasty in any criticism I might make, so I spent quite a number of laps getting to know the car. The V6 cylinder engine was a delight, revving freely and smoothly to its limit but I was rather disappointed in power output for it wasn't quite the equal of the V8 Coventry-Climax and BRM engines being used by the opposition. The gearbox was equally delightful with the best, slickest and most positive gear change I'd ever used. Sadly the handling wasn't very good, severe understeer being the first problem. This was reduced but still I wasn't happy and when we went further, lurid oversteer developed. I felt one of the problems was the Borrani wire wheels which were flexing. The thing that most impressed me was how good the car felt in the wet. Always controllable, it felt safe, never likely to spring a surprise and get the better of me. In the end the best I could do was fourth place. (*Thoroughbred and Classic Cars*, December 1988, pp. 105–6).

Graham Hill's BRM sneaked past Jim Clark at the line for their famous finish, with Surtees third and Ireland a lap down. The great Hill–Clark battles had begun but Ferrari was struggling. It is an interesting side note

Ireland leads Clark in the Silverstone International Trophy. Ireland finished fourth, Clark second. (BRDC Archive)

that around this time, *Autosport* photographer and writer David Phipps had an unaccompanied and largely unauthorised tour of the Ferrari factory at Maranello. Although he was told the four valves per cylinder head was the central development in the engine department, his snooping was particularly revealing in relation to the front suspension of the 156, where he could see that nothing had been done to deal with front-end dive under braking; thus there was a high degree of negative camber, even with an anti-roll bar, and the roll centre was relatively high. The rear suspension was still set for considerable camber change during cornering, which Phipps saw as an indication that advances in the handling had not gone very far (*Autosport*, 25 May 1962).

20 May was the beginning of another weekend with two F1 races. Ferrari sent the car Ireland had used at Silverstone to Naples for Willy Mairesse (0001) and Bandini was back in 0006 which he had used at Pau; chassis 0003, 0004, and 0007 went to the Dutch Grand Prix at Zandvoort for Rodriguez, Hill and Baghetti. While Rodriguez had his Pau car, and Baghetti the car Hill drove at Aintree, Hill was down to drive 0004. But that was the chassis number of von Trips's car which surely had been written off at Monza. Even Doug Nye's work on chassis numbers doesn't seem to question this apparent discrepancy. While a new chassis may have been built using either 0004 from von Trips's car or designated as a 1962 version 0004, the author suspects Hill may in fact have been driving his Monza-winning car, 0002, though it does seem that 0004 appeared twice more in 1962, both times driven by Mairesse.

Down in the south of Italy, Bandini was showing something of his skill by grabbing pole by two-tenths of a second from Mairesse. Bandini led the field, such as it was, for not quite half the race before the Belgian, who had been right on the Italian's tail, took over and went on to win, thus securing the second of his only two F1 wins. Keith Greene, the English privateer, was a solid third, another Italian newcomer, Mario Abate, was fourth and Ian Burgess fifth.

Back in the coastal dunes of Zandvoort, things seemed to be going from bad to worse for Phil Hill. His car appeared sporting the inboard-mounted gearbox and the wider track which seemed to get a new lease on life after it had been suggested by Innes Ireland. According to Nye (1979), Hill must have been very irritated by the notion that Chiti hadn't wanted to instal the wide track in 1961 but now Forghieri was using it. This didn't help Hill's relationship with Forghieri. According to Hill: 'My car was demonstrably slower on the straights, but they would not admit to the obvious. . . . The handling was improved but the wind resistance increased. It was so bad that the car was down several hundred revs on the straight. I had to slipstream guys like Rodriguez to keep up with traffic (Grayson, 1975, p. 234).

It also has to be remembered that Zandvoort was following close on the heels of the Targa Florio (6 May) where Hill had had a high-speed crash in practice with his 268SP, the 2.6-litre V8, when the throttle jammed wide open. John Godfrey describes the event in vivid detail (1990). In effect, Hill reported to Dragoni what had occurred, and Dragoni made it clear that he suspected Hill was lying to get out of responsibility for the accident. Dragoni immediately headed back to the car, and so did Hill, but

by another route. Getting there first with his mechanic Dino Pignatti, Hill looked down to see the throttle slides jammed open. Dragoni was furious and though he didn't accuse Hill of jamming the throttle open, the effect was the same. It seems this was the point at which Dragoni openly started to tell people that Hill had lost his nerve and had been 'psychologically impressioned' by von Trips's death. He certainly told Hill himself that.

The extra cross links that had been added to the rear suspension to reduce toe steer had now been removed from all three cars, but this wasn't as problematic for the Ferraris as the arrival of Colin Chapman's monocoque Lotus 25 driven by Jim Clark. Lotus driver Trevor Taylor told the author how the Dutch Grand Prix unfolded and how he was about to 'renew his acquaintance' with a 'sharknose' Ferrari after his close call at Brussels with Mairesse:

In some ways Formula 1 was my biggest disaster and I'll admit it to this day. I finished up being a development engineer . . . I was testing all the new suspension and gearboxes and anything that broke, broke on me before the car was handed on. At Zandvoort, I should have been driving the new 25 which had just come out, but Jimmy [Clark] was so competitive that when he saw it he wanted to drive it. He probably would have won if he had stayed in the 24, but instead we swapped and I finished second, my best result in a Grand Prix. The thing that amazed me in that race, and there were some breakdowns, but the amazing moment in my first 'proper' Grand Prix was when I overtook Phil Hill. I was going down the straight and I looked over and I remember it upset

Willy Mairesse, pictured here, led Bandini to a Ferrari 1–2 at Naples in a non-championship race on the same day as the Dutch Grand Prix, 1962. (Gunter Molter)

me, and I thought 'he's a champion'. When Phil overtook me at Aintree I remember thinking: 'I wish I was half as good as he is'. Then the tables reversed and I overtook him, and I was second because he had been second. It was a pretty big moment for me . . . Graham Hill first, me second, and Phil Hill third. It was lucky in some ways because near the beginning Rodriguez had a big spin and Brabham hit him and I just missed them, not like in Belgium where I did get hit.

Not only did the new Lotus 25 appear in Holland, but Gurney and Bonnier each had the new flat-8 air-cooled Porsches. After three practice sessions and much fiddling with the camber at the rear, which didn't seem to be doing much good, Hill's Ferrari was still a second ahead of Baghetti and Rodriguez was struggling somewhat, this being his first time at Zandvoort. Nevertheless, Hill had qualified down in ninth behind the Lotus, Cooper, BRM, Porsche and Lola brigade with Baghetti and Rodriguez on the next row. Phil Hill drove a very hard race given the car's handling, and had pulled up to second in the later stages until Taylor got past him. Rodriguez had one too many spins and ended in the catch fencing, while Baghetti drove to a steady fourth. So while the cars didn't feel competitive, they were still getting the results, in large part because of Hill's gritty driving and Baghetti's unruffled style.

Just a week after Zandvoort and a week before Monaco, Phil Hill and Olivier Gendebien raised the Ferrari camp's morale by taking a rousing victory at the Nürburgring 1000 Kilometre race in the rear-engined 246SP, while the potent 4-litre Ferrari GTO in the hands of Mike Parkes and Mairesse followed them into second. The bigger prototype class cars in this sports car race had to put up with being considerably frightened when Jim Clark in the minuscule 1.5-litre Lotus 23 led for a dozen laps. But Hill had demonstrated, if any demo was needed, that he was just as much at home on mountainous circuits as anywhere else, and the Hill/Gendebien duo chalked up another reminder of how they had become one of the best endurance pairings ever.

In retrospect, Phil Hill views Monaco as his best race of 1962: 'There had been some developments on the car, and Forghieri was working very hard on it. I think if I had had another lap or two, I would have been able to at least try to get past McLaren.' John Cooper, who entered McLaren's Cooper, told the author that he was sure Hill was going to get past McLaren 'because Hill was catching him at an enormous rate'.

Bearing in mind the reputation Ferrari had to live up to after the 1961 race, and still wanting to take victory in the principality, SEFAC Ferrari sent five cars to Monaco for qualifying. Sixteen cars would start, ten places being given to the main teams. Ferrari nominated Hill and Mairesse to drive, so Bandini and Rodriguez had to fight it out among themselves to get one of the remaining six grid spots. The choice of Mairesse rather than Bandini was interesting, and if Dragoni had power behind the scenes at Ferrari, it wasn't showing when the drive went to the Belgian over the Italian.

Chassis 0007 was allocated to Hill, 0001 to Bandini and the still slightly mysterious 0004 to Mairesse. All were now 120-degree engined

Lotus boss Colin Chapman in Clark's car as work is carried out during the practice session at Zandvoort, 1962. (Paul Meis)

Above: Rodriguez shortly before tangling with both Jack Brabham and the catch fencing at Zandvoort, 1962. (National Motor Museum) *Below*: This fine side view captures the lines of the 'sharknose'. Phil Hill is bolt upright as usual. (Paul Meis)

Above: The 120-degree engine. In the rear bodywork the carb covers can be seen with scoops just behind them to bring cool air to the brakes. The coil springs were now more steeply inclined than they had been.

Right: The clutch remained behind the differential throughout the history of the 'sharknose'. (Jim Gleave/Atlantic Art)

cars, with wide track rear suspension and rear-mounted gearbox, though all three had the 1961 location of the coil/damper top mounts which meant the suspension had more negative camber at Monaco than anywhere else in 1962. A 65-degree car was brought for Ricardo Rodriguez, possibly 0006, while the fifth car, in which Phil Hill practised, was presumably new chassis 0009, carrying the inboard gearbox. This was described as a 1962 car while Rodriguez' was a 1961 car. Jenkinson describes Phil Hill racing the car with the cut down windscreen, while Nye (1979) says this was the practice car.

When practice was over, Mairesse was on the second row in a splendid fourth place, with Hill two rows back in ninth and Bandini next to him. Clark had driven the first sub-1 minute 36 seconds lap. Graham Hill and Bruce McLaren joined him on the front row. Rodriguez had failed to qualify.

The 'sharknose' line-up for the 1962 Monaco Grand Prix. Bandini is talking to his mechanics. (Archive von Trips/Fodisch)

Right: Bandini's 120-degree car had Perspex covers on the carburettors for the Monaco Grand Prix in 1962. *Below*: The Ferrari line-up in the totally unprotected pit area at Monaco, which was on the other side of the wall from the previous years. (Jim Gleave/Atlantic Art)

Above: The first lap of the Monaco Grand Prix in 1962 and Mairesse has forced his way to the front. *Below*: Mairesse (40) forces Graham Hill (10) and Dan Gurney wide as he attempts to hold the lead, Monaco, 1962. (Jim Gleave/Atlantic Art)

All hell broke loose at the start as 'Wild Willy' put his foot down and shot away, shoving both Clark and Hill aside. Mairesse steamed into the Gasworks hairpin far too fast, causing mayhem behind him. As Graham Hill, McLaren and Clark headed down the straight, Mairesse caught his slide and chased after them, but by then Gurney, Ginther and Trintignant had suffered damage and were out, and Ireland and Taylor were limping towards the pits for repairs. Ginther thought the opening lap crash had been his fault and that his throttle had stuck but that was probably because everyone had braked so hard in front of him! Movie producer and director Roger Corman was making a motor racing film that year, *The Young Racers*, which caught the opening laps and Mairesse's lunge into the first corner beautifully, as well as recording the multiple crash.

Mairesse managed to spin again at the Station hairpin and dropped back, but Phil Hill had done a fine job of sneaking through into third, with Clark stuck back in sixth. Hill had a quick spin on lap 12. Up to lap 56 the race was all about whether Clark could catch Graham Hill – but then his gearbox packed up. Phil Hill kept his head down, driving purposefully and working to stay in touch with Graham Hill, McLaren

Jim Clark goes inside Jack Brabham (22) as Bonnier (2) brakes, and Tony Maggs (16) forces Bandini to the outside, Monaco, 1962. (Jim Gleave/Atlantic Art)

Mairesse just after a first lap spin, Monaco, 1962. (Jim Gleave/Atlantic Art)

Bandini drives to a lonely third 80 seconds behind Phil Hill, Monaco, 1962. (Jim Gleave/Atlantic Art)

and Brabham, whom he finally worried into a spin at the Casino. As the BRM got smokier, the 'flat out' sign came out to Phil on lap 84, and then on lap 93 the BRM blew. Phil Hill was 12 seconds behind with five laps to go, then 11 seconds, then 8, then 7, and as they started the last lap the gap was 5 seconds. Hill had driven beautifully but was still 1.3 seconds adrift at the finish. Lorenzo Bandini was now up in third and on the same lap as Phil Hill and McLaren. Sadly, except for a further non-championship win a bit later, that was as good as it was going to get.

The 2000 Guineas for F1 cars was run on 11 June at the 1.3 mile Mallory Park circuit in England. Phil Hill had been entered but the car was not sent, and the entry was of much lower quality than had been promoted. Surtees won from Brabham and Graham Hill after Clark retired in a race that only saw one change of position between laps 28 and 75. Oddly enough, there was another F1 race the same day at Crystal Palace in London which went to the Lotus 24 of Innes Ireland; Roy Salvadori was second.

Two weeks after Monaco came the Belgian Grand Prix at Spa, where Phil Hill had led the Ferrari 1–2–3–4 the previous year. Although the new Porsche failed to turn up, this was going to be the season's first real high-speed test. It would determine how much the V8s had caught up with Ferrari. Four cars were sent to try to protect the Ferrari record at Spa: chassis 0009 for Hill, 0004 for Mairesse, 0001 for Baghetti, and 0003 for Rodriguez. All four were listed as 1962 cars, and all had 120-degree engines. It is possible that 0001 and 0003 were replacement chassis built for 1962, though in fact there was not much on them that differed drastically from the earlier cars. One way of telling the difference was the type and number of air scoops on the car, but by now, some bodywork was being used interchangeably between older and newer chassis. Three of these cars – 0001, 0004 and 0009 – had new front wishbones with base pivots that were more easily adjustable. All had the wider rear wishbones and 0003 had a rear anti-roll bar. There wasn't a four valves per cylinder head or inboard gearbox in sight.

During practice much effort went into trying to reduce drag. Phil Hill was happy with the handling but power was clearly lacking. The Perspex carb covers and air scoops to the brakes were removed and Hill was the first to go under 4 minutes, but still slower than the previous year. His car leaked oil in the second practice and Baghetti had a big fright after the mechanics overlooked the fastenings on the engine cover, which blew off in the daunting uphill Eau Rouge corner, spinning Baghetti into the fence. The damage, however, was reparable, and leather straps sprouted on the rear covers.

The race turned out to be another classic high-speed chase, with Jim Clark moving up from mid-field to battle with Lotus team-mate Trevor Taylor, Mairesse in the Ferrari, Graham Hill and Bruce McLaren. This struggle continued to the halfway stage when McLaren and Hill dropped back and Clark moved out in front, but by then the race average was as high as the previous year's fastest lap. The cars went round at an average of over 130mph. Baghetti made a stop and then retired with ignition problems. Phil Hill and Ricardo Rodriguez provided the other excitement,

Willy Mairesse and Team
Manager Eugenio Dragoni
confer before practice for the
Belgian Grand Prix at Spa,
1962. (Author's Collection)

passing and re-passing in sixth and seventh, then fifth and sixth. Hill
recalled the race:

> I remember it but I don't recall it being that much of a battle. We had
> been told by the Dunlop people that we were going to lose the inside of
> our rear tyres which we did because there was too much camber. We
> lost all the tread on the inside. I don't know what Ricardo was doing
> but I wasn't battling. I was trying to keep going and save the tyres.

Anyone either present at the race or who has seen films of it might
question this, as the two 'sharknose' cars ran so closely lap after lap, both
driven very smoothly compared with what was going on up at the front.
Rodriguez certainly seemed to be trying as Hill went down the inside at the
hairpin for the last time and led across the finishing line by inches, and
there certainly wasn't any evidence of team orders. In spite of what seemed
a good performance, Hill was still unhappy with the speed of the car:
'Remember, there were two cars in '62, there was mine and then there was
all the rest, those were the same as the year before. If there had been some
way of combining the virtues of both it would have been a world beater.'

Above: Hill leads Rodriguez in their race long battle for third and fourth positions, Belgian Grand Prix, 1962. *Below*: Ricardo Rodriguez brakes heavily for La Source. (Jim Gleave/Atlantic Art)

Hill leads Rodriguez from Blanchimont as they return towards the pits at Spa in 1962. Baghetti follows behind. (Jim Gleave/Atlantic Art)

With six laps to go, Taylor and Mairesse were still at it, and at the fast left-hander at Blanchimont the two cars touched. The author asked Trevor Taylor about the accusation levelled at him and Mairesse that they were driving over their heads:

Were we driving over our heads? Were we ever! To be honest, I made a mistake because I was leading the race and I braked so hard at La Source that I locked up and spun it. Jimmy [Clark] went by, and Mairesse caught me. I'll tell you something, I never changed gears on that circuit except at the hairpin and then up the gears down the old pit straight. It was fourth at the long left-hander past Eau Rouge but all the rest of it was top gear, even at the end of the Masta Straight. Once Mairesse got on my tail, I just couldn't shake him off. I was pulling him around the circuit. Things were getting tough, the tyres were going, there was oil on the track. We were about a mile from the hairpin at Blanchimont and Mairesse was so close to me, and I think he saved my life. I arrived at that left-hand corner and I was out of gear, he had touched me. The marshals said he had hit me up the back and it came out of gear so I started to go around. But instead of him following me, which was the natural thing, he came up the inside and knocked me straight. He shot off and knocked down some trees and a telegraph pole, and I ended up in the ditch with the telegraph pole across the car behind my head. I had these dark glasses and I thought I was blind, but it was all this muddy water on the lenses! Then I saw the fire in his car, but he had been thrown out. I went to see him in the hospital and

Above: Willy Mairesse as he attempts to catch Trevor Taylor, Spa, 1962. *Below*: Mairesse closes on Taylor's Lotus as they exit La Source. (Jim Gleave/Atlantic Art)

Above: Mairesse has managed to get past Taylor as they head down past the pits at Spa. *Below*: Mairesse stretches the lead momentarily. (Jim Gleave/Atlantic Art)

he said, 'Great race . . . one of those things.' I was always getting messed up with Mairesse. He spun and hit me in the Brussels race.

While Taylor and Mairesse escaped with fairly minor injuries, Clark ran out the winner, and Graham Hill came home second, with Hill and Rodriguez third and fourth. Though Phil Hill's view was that 'the wide-track car still couldn't get out of its own way' (Grayson, 1975, p. 234), he had nevertheless managed to keep himself second in the championship points with 14 points to Graham Hill's 16. In his film *The Young Racers*, Roger Corman captured wonderful shots of both the Taylor/Mairesse and Hill/Rodriguez dices, though sadly it was a terrible movie! The makers advertised in *Autosport* for film of the Taylor/Mairesse accident, and got it, so the finished product included a shot of the Ferrari burning away.

Although Phil Hill had overheard Dragoni reporting to Enzo Ferrari after Spa that 'your champion has done nothing', his competitive spirit was undeterred as he and Gendebien scored a fine win at Le Mans in the Ferrari TRI/330, the 4-litre car.

A general industrial strike in Italy, which particularly affected the metal workers, provided Ferrari with a good reason for staying away from the non-championship race at Rheims on 2 July. The event was won by

Mairesse touched Taylor just before this point at Blanchimont on the following lap and they crashed. (Jim Gleave/Atlantic Art)

McLaren. Nor did the team go to the French Grand Prix at Rouen on 8 July. This same industrial strike didn't seem to affect getting the cars to Le Mans, however.

Gurney gave the flat-8 Porsche its famous win at Rouen ahead of Tony Maggs in a Cooper. Gurney also had a win at the non-championship race at Solitude on 15 July. As an aside, Nye (1975) reported that Signor Ferrari was unhappy with Phil Hill for driving a Scuderia Filipinetti Lotus 24 at Solitude and Rheims – the interesting part is this never happened at either race!

With neither Clark nor Graham Hill scoring in the French Grand Prix, there might have been a chance for some more Ferrari championship points. However, the performance of the car at Aintree in the British Grand Prix on 21 July meant that any points gained in France would have counted for little, as both Graham Hill and Clark scored and Phil Hill had his first non-finish in the 'sharknose' for two seasons. Hill was only twelfth in practice in chassis 0007, the 120-degree car with inboard gearbox which he had tried in practice at Monaco. The other two Ferrari entries were withdrawn. In the race Hill got up to ninth before the engine went rough and retired with a faulty distributor, though the handling had been 'unpredictable'. Clark disappeared into the distance to win.

With four grand prix races left at the Nürburgring, Monza, Watkins Glen and in South Africa, and with rumours and stories all year that the 'new' Ferrari air-cooled V8 designed in conjunction with the Gilera motorbike concern would soon appear, a mixed reaction greeted the opening of the Ferrari transporter in the Nürburgring paddock for the 5 August race. Out came Hill's machine, 0007 according to its chassis plate, though Ferrari had it listed as 0002. However, it certainly looked

The cockpit of Phil Hill's car at Nürburgring for the German Grand Prix, 1962. (Jim Gleave/Atlantic Art)

Mechanic Giulio Borsari works on Giancarlo Baghetti's chassis 0001. (Jim Gleave/Atlantic Art)

The throttle return gets attention on one of the 120-degree engine cars, Nürburgring, 1962. (Jim Gleave/Atlantic Art)

Hill's car with another variation on the scoops to bring air to the rear brakes. (Jim Gleave/Atlantic Art)

like the Aintree car with inboard gearbox, and it certainly seemed to feel like it: 'It was absolutely diabolical at the Nürburgring. I could not hold the car on the road and the shock absorbers were just gone. That was the worst it had been.'

Baghetti was listed by Ferrari as being in 0007 but in fact his was probably the car he drove at Spa, 0001. Rodriguez, much to his disappointment, had a 1961 spec 65-degree machine, probably 0006 which had raced at Spa – so much for the promises made at the press day!

Bandini, however, was in a new car, chassis 0008 – not the original prototype that carried this number, but a wholly new car. Indeed there were many things different about it, but it didn't have the V8, nor did it have the four valves per cylinder. It was referred to as a 156/62/P, and it was the chassis built for the four-valve engine, though in reality the power unit was an earlier 120-degree engine from 1961. Significantly, it was *not* a 'sharknose' . The unique nose had disappeared and had been replaced with one which, according to Tanner (1989), made it look like a contemporary Lotus or Cooper. However, the new nose was much more like the single aperture openings on the 1960 and 1961 British cars and the original Ferrari rear-engined prototype, rather than the much smaller current nose opening of the other 1962 cars.

Above: The first appearance of the non-'sharknose' 156 at the Nürburgring, with Bandini driving and Mauro Forghieri talking to him. English journalist Denis Jenkinson is perusing the new car, chassis 0008. *Right*: The new 156 featured much-altered carburettor covers and brake-cooling intakes. (Jim Gleave/Atlantic Art)

Rear view of 0008 with open tail section and shortened exhaust pipes. (Jim Gleave/Atlantic Art)

Some structural changes had been made to the chassis in order to reduce flexing. The pedals were further forward, and the driver's seat more inclined to reduce overall frontal area. Water was now carried via the chassis longerons, the fuel tanks had been relocated and reshaped, and the suspension was altered at the back to shift the weight distribution, though the changes at the front were limited. The rear body area had lost the grille openings, and the carburettor coverings were bulges beaten out of the rear section, with scoops fitted just over and behind them to bring air to the rear brakes. Phil Hill tried the car in practice but found that he slid out of the new seat, and so gave it back to Bandini.

Ferraris didn't get out in the first practice and the team looked very disorganised in the second, while Clark put in a good time and then Gurney rattled everyone by doing 8 minutes 47 seconds. None of the Ferraris made under 9 minutes: Rodriguez was fastest with 9 minutes 14.2 seconds; Bandini was 25 seconds slower. If Forghieri was pinning his hopes on this race, it didn't look very encouraging. On Saturday Clark went faster in the wet than the Ferraris had gone in the dry, and even Rodriguez' fastest Ferrari time was slower than deBeaufort in his Porsche!

On Sunday 360,000 wet fans watched the start. Gurney led Graham Hill and an amazing Phil Hill up from twelfth in one lap. Phil and Rodriguez were up among the leading six for many laps. Bandini fell off at the Karussel, damaging the new car but managing to get it back to the pits. Phil Hill had to stop for a new visor; by the halfway stage his shock absorbers were not working, the car was impossible to control and he retired. Rodriguez drove as hard as he could to sixth, Baghetti carefully to tenth. Graham Hill won by 22.5 seconds from Surtees, Gurney and Clark. Jack Brabham retired his new Brabham-Climax on lap 9.

Early August saw two Scandinavian races, Masten Gregory's Lotus-BRM winning at Karlskoga and Brabham in a Lotus beating Gregory at Roskilde. Then, on 19 August, the Mediterranean Grand Prix was run on the ultra-fast Enna circuit around Lake Pergusa in Sicily. Bandini took pole position in 0009, which Hill had used at Spa, and Baghetti had 0003, which had been raced by Rodriguez at the Belgian circuit, but the two Italians couldn't keep the cars as close together as the American and the Mexican had at Spa in the same cars. Bandini beat a field of privateers at an average of 129mph, with Baghetti 32 seconds behind and Abate third.

Jim Clark in his Lotus makes an amusing point to his mechanic. (Jim Gleave/Atlantic Art)

Above: The wet start for the German Grand Prix in 1962 with Hill (1), Rodriguez (3) and Bandini (4) spread across the third row. (Porsche) *Left*: Baghetti struggled on to a distant tenth place in the 1962 German Grand Prix. (Gunter Molter)

Bandini leads Tony Magg's Cooper (10) and Baghetti in he early stages of the German Grand Prix, 1962. (Gunter Molter)

Bandini crashed shortly after this photograph was taken but managed to get back to the pits. (Gunter Molter)

Hill retired from the German Grand Prix in 1962 after what he described as his worst race in the 'sharknose'. (Gunter Molter)

Jim Clark beat Graham Hill in the F1 Gold Cup race at Oulton Park on 1 September, and Stirling Moss, who was still recuperating from his injuries, got a huge reception from the crowd. But he was now clearly a spectator.

Ferrari dispatched five cars for what would be its final race of the year, the Italian Grand Prix at Monza on 16 September. This time the race was to be held on the shorter road circuit without the banking. This race marked Phil Hill's departure from Ferrari, and while he now refuses to discuss the details, he said some years after the event (Grayson, 1975, p. 236) that 'they had screwed up my engine to the point where even they recognised it'. The bitterness over this episode is obviously clearly remembered. Hill had been saying all season that his car was not as good as the others, particularly at the fast circuits. Ferrari, or Dragoni specifically, said it was Hill that was not quick. The argument here is that Enzo Ferrari needed a scapegoat for the cars' poor performance, because if the cars were not up to scratch, then neither was he. Hill feels he was that scapegoat: 'It handled better that year, but it was much slower on the straights. Over the tighter circuits I was able to hold my own and, in fact, I was running a close second for the championship with Graham Hill as late as Belgium in June. Of course, Graham went on to win as things got worse and worse for us. But there was nothing I could have done to change the results.' (Nolan, 1996, p. 210)

Five Ferraris showed up for practice. Hill had a central gearbox car, chassis 0002, the same machine that he had driven at the Nürburgring. Mairesse had 0008, the experimental car which Bandini ran in Germany and still with the non-'sharknose' front section – it had been revealed that this car was a good bit lighter than the others. Rodriguez was out again, this time in the 120-degree 0007, with Baghetti in 0003 with a 120-degree engine, and finally Bandini in 0006, who had been relegated to the older 65-degree car, even though he had won at Enna. It seems the chassis plates on 0002 and 0007 had been sorted.

Mairesse, back after his huge Spa crash, wasted no time in driving straight into the back of Gregory who was out on a warm-up lap. All the Ferraris were suffering major understeer problems and it seemed nothing could cure them, but to his credit Mairesse was the fastest of the five, getting on to the fourth row. There were comments about how much this was down to his skill and how much it was the result of a total lack of sense – by now Mairesse certainly worried a number of other drivers. Clark was under Phil Hill's circuit record and the first several rows of the grid were much closer than usual at Monza.

This had promised to be a race between Graham Hill and Jim Clark for the championship, but Clark stopped early with transmission woes and Hill drove away. The field split into two groups, with all the Ferraris in the second. Bandini dropped right back, and then Phil Hill couldn't hang on to the other three red cars and was lapped by halfway. Rodriguez, Baghetti and Mairesse fought hard with Bonnier until Rodriguez' engine went flat and finally stopped. Then Baghetti had a spin. Mairesse was left to chase hard. Hill stopped for fuel on lap 83 and got told off by Dragoni for doing so. Then Bandini came in as well because he needed fuel. Mairesse lost a good third place to McLaren near the end as the BRMs of

Graham Hill and Ginther were 1–2. Baghetti plodded on to fifth and Phil Hill was eleventh.

On 21 September, Enzo Ferrari sent the following letter to Phil Hill, Ricardo Rodriguez, Lorenzo Bandini and Giancarlo Baghetti:

Gentlemen: The industrial situation has once more rendered it impossible to finalize our racing programme, whereby we had hoped to produce our four new Formula 1 cars for Monza. Without the cooperation of the workers, for reasons stemming from a national not a local dispute which began last March, we are forced to withdraw from further competition. Within the limits imposed by reduced working hours, we shall continue to work on the prototype Formula 1 car and hope that we shall later benefit from this. Meanwhile, if you wish, you are at liberty to compete in other marques for this season's remaining races, with the sole proviso that you respect our contracts with Dunlop, Shell, Marchal and Ferodo. We would like to thank you for your help during this season and we are sorry that we were unable to put at

Enzo Ferrari talks to Dragoni with Bandini in the background. This was one of Ferrari's rare visits to practice at Monza for the Italian Grand Prix and it took place on Saturday 15 September 1962. (Jim Gleave/Atlantic Art)

Above: Rodriguez (4) and Baghetti (2) at full speed past the pits in the Italian Grand Prix at Monza, 1962. *Below*: Rodriguez leads Mairesse in the non-'sharknose' 156, Monza. (Jerry Sloniger)

your disposal Formula 1 cars as successful as our G.T., sports and experimental machines.

Rodriguez' race ends in engine failure, Monza, 1962. (Jerry Sloniger)

None of this came as much of a surprise to the drivers or to the more discerning motoring press, though it was a sign of the times that not much editorial space was given to discussing it. Denis Jenkinson saw it as Ferrari's annual excuse not to send cars abroad after Maranello's position had been settled, though rumours that Phil Hill had been fired were already getting round. Ricardo Rodriguez had already been talking to Count Volpi and the Serenissima Team about driving either a Serenissima F1 or the new ATS in 1963. Rodriguez told his friend 'Flacco' Barrios that he was surprised that 'Enzo Ferrari would lie in writing', and that he was also thinking about retiring after the non-championship Mexican Grand Prix.

The conditions imposed by Ferrari wouldn't make it easy for any of the drivers to get another opportunity to race that season. Mairesse had been left out of the equation because he was being retained as a test driver.

EPILOGUE

On 7 October 1962 Jim Clark kept his championship hopes alive by winning the United States Grand Prix at Watkins Glen, his Lotus 25 leading Graham Hill's BRM P57 across the line by 9 seconds. To many people's surprise, Phil Hill appeared in Jo Bonnier's works Porsche flat-8 in one of the Saturday practice sessions because Bonnier was suffering from a bad back. It wasn't a serious effort, though, and was arranged just in case Bonnier couldn't drive on the Sunday, but he had recovered by then.

Ricardo and Pedro Rodriguez won the Paris 1,000-Kilometres on 21 October in a NART Ferrari 250 GTO, driving a flawless race to finish a lap ahead of John Surtees and Mike Parkes in another GTO. A few weeks later, Ricardo, having walked up to Rob Walker at Monza and asked if he could drive one of Walker's cars for the first Mexican Grand Prix, was killed at the end of the practice session. He had put yet another car he had never driven before on provisional pole position. It was clear, even at Monza, that Ferrari was not going to send a car to Mexico.

On 29 December, Graham Hill snatched the 1962 World Championship by winning the South African Grand Prix at East London, when Jim Clark dropped out after the failure of an oil ring.

Former World Champion Phil Hill, along with Ferrari team-mate Giancarlo Baghetti, went to rejoin old friends Chiti and Tavoni at the new ATS team. This was another emotional and unfortunate decision for both of them, although the ATS project looked promising at the time. It is somewhat ironic that both the team's cars are now back in historic racing. Hill later went to Cooper, which was not having a successful time, but he continued to have a number of good results in a range of sports cars for some years, and is still active in historic racing today.

Baghetti rather stuttered to the end of his career, got involved in publishing as a photographer and was refused an interview by Enzo Ferrari, who held him in some contempt just for asking. Baghetti died just a few years ago, having had cancer and then a heart attack. Enzo Ferrari died in 1988 at the age of ninety, and since that time very few writers have got to grips with the intrigues and plots that dominated his life in racing. In spite of the way many drivers and other employees were treated by him, however, very few would deny that he was a great man.

Lorenzo Bandini rejoined Ferrari, and after John Surtees left in 1966, looked as if he might become one of Ferrari's best drivers, but he was killed in a Ferrari at Monaco in 1967. Willy Mairesse stayed with the

Formula 1 team at the beginning of 1963, was replaced by Scarfiotti after suffering burns at Le Mans, returned later in the season and had a big crash at the Nürburgring. He was again replaced, this time by Bandini. He never drove in F1 again, but took part in several sports car races and suffered several crashes, his last at Le Mans in 1968. Realising he was not going to get another good drive, he killed himself in an Ostend hotel room in 1969.

Richie Ginther had a few reasonable seasons at BRM, then helped develop the Honda F1 car and won at Mexico in 1965. In 1967, he was waiting to practise at Indy when he decided it was time to retire. After living in a motor home in remote areas of California for some years, he came back on to the scene briefly in 1989 but died of heart failure that year.

Olivier Gendebien retired from racing in 1962, lived in the USA for a number of years, and died in 1998 after a lengthy illness, long after he and Phil Hill had established themselves as one of the most successful long-distance partnerships of all time.

Of the other significant 'sharknose' team members, only Mauro Forghieri continues to work as a consultant engineer to a number of projects including his own ARAL Company, located between Modena and Maranello. Carlo Chiti eventually returned to Alfa Romeo to develop their successful sports car programme from 1967 to 1977 and saw Alfa return to Grand Prix racing. He was still working on a number of projects at the time of his death in the 1990s. Romulo Tavoni lives in retirement in a small Italian village, having remained active in motor racing administration for many years after leaving Ferrari. Eugenio Dragoni died in the 1970s after several years of working with Enzo Ferrari before he too got the push.

And what about the cars? This book started out to consider the Ferrari 156 'sharknose', but it would be inaccurate to imply that the 'sharknose' version was synonymous with the 156 model, because it wasn't. The 'sharknose' was really the term that was popularly given to the cars of 1961 and 1962, which were identified by their striking and unique front end and became famous for winning Grand Prix races during that short period of time. The sheer number of 'sharknose' cars that appeared at some races caught the imagination of racing enthusiasts and many ordinary people as well. Their reputation was bolstered by the mystique of Ferrari and the drivers of the time, particularly the aristocratic Count Wolfgang von Trips and the gritty, tough and intelligent American World Champion Phil Hill.

The 156 – in so far as the 15 referred to a 1.5-litre engine and 6 designated a six-cylinder engine – persisted as the designation for the F1 Ferraris of 1963 and the first race of 1964. It was then replaced by the 158, the eight-cylinder car, still water-cooled, and long delayed. Ferrari had only been fifth in the constructors' table in 1962 and rose to fourth in 1963. Surtees finished fourth in the drivers' championship in 1963, whereas Phil Hill had dropped to sixth by the end of 1962. John Surtees was testing a revised version of 0008, the non-'sharknose' car, with a much smaller nose aperture than the one that had appeared at the Ring and Monza. This was in November 1962. Surtees did win the German Grand Prix at the Nürburgring in 1963 but it was not a brilliant season: Mauro Forghieri was still on a steep learning curve that would eventually lead to much better days.

In Italy at the time it was something of a tradition to sell ex-works Grand Prix cars on to amateurs, but Ferrari rarely if ever countenanced this policy. Surviving cars had no significance to Enzo Ferrari, even victorious ones, and he was often quoted as saying that the only important racing car was the one he was building tomorrow. At one time he even kept a collection of damaged parts on display to warn factory employees what they had to avoid in the future. Hence, all eight Ferrari 'sharknose' cars of 1961 and 1962 – eight in total, or possibly nine, as some 1961 cars became 1962 cars and there remain uncertainties about some chassis – were destroyed, either in races or at the order of Enzo Ferrari. Sometimes the engines were removed, but not always, and they were simply scrapped not far from the factory. At Maserati, the old cars remained in the yard behind the factory for years, but Ferraris were taken away and destroyed, a policy Alfa Romeo also adhered to for some time.

Thus, in spite of many years of speculation and hunting, not one original Ferrari 'sharknose' has ever reappeared. There have been rumours but none has emerged, even in this age when huge values are placed on historic racing cars.

British rock star and racing driver Chris Rea caused a sensation when he commissioned a copy of the 'sharknose' to star in the film he produced about his own experience of 'La Passione'. Although this car attracted a lot of attention and still does, it was not a detailed and accurate reproduction. However, a machine is now being built using the remains of an original engine block and gearbox. During the period that the 'sharknose' raced, several other companies built cars with a twin nostril, none of them particularly successful. These included at least one Formula 1 car and several Formula Juniors, including the Wainer and the Stanguellini. None of these captured the imagination like the Ferrari did, and neither have the recreations constructed since.

A number of enthusiasts have tried to recapture the period when one racing car manufacturer had the foresight to see the way the sport might go in the future. Ferrari produced a beautiful and rapid racing machine, and put it into the hands of some of the most skilled *piloti* of the time. But that was another era and the age of the 'sharknose' will never return.

BIBLIOGRAPHY

BOOKS

Biolchini, Romano, *Quelli Dei Box E Dintorni*, ROMBI Edizioni, Milan, 1999

Casucci, Piero, *Chiti Grand Prix*, International Automobilia Publishing Group, Milan, 1987

——, *Enzo Ferrari: Fifty Years of Greatness*, Haynes Publishing, Somerset, 1982

Ferrari, Enzo, *Ferrari: Piloti, che gente . . .*, Conti Editore, Bologna, 1985

Fodisch, Jorg-Thomas and C. Dewitz, *Trips–Bilder eines Lebens*, Edition Fodisch, Bonn, 2000

——, and C. and R. Louis, *Trips-Erinnerungen an ein Idol*, Heel, Konigswinter, Germany, 1998

Gauld, Graham, *Jim Clark – The Legend Lives On*, Haynes Publishing, Somerset, 1992

——, *Modena Racing Memories*, MBI Publishing, Wisconsin, 1999

Godfrey, John, *Ferrari Dino SPs*, Patrick Stephens Ltd., Wellingborough, 1990

Grayson, Stan (ed.), *Ferrari: The Man, The Machines*, Automobile Quarterly Publications, New Jersey, 1975

Henry, Alan, *Ferrari: The Grand Prix Cars*, Hazleton Publishing, Surrey, 1989

——, *Fifty Years of Ferrari*, Haynes Publishing, Somerset, 1997

——, *Formula One Driver By Driver*, Crowood Press, Wiltshire, 1992

Hayhoe, David and D. Holland, *Grand Prix Databook 1997*, Duke Marketing, Isle of Man, 1996

Hodges, David, *A–Z of Formula Racing Cars 1945–1990*, Bay View Books, Devon, 1998

Lawrence, Mike, *Grand Prix Cars 1945–65*, Motor Racing Publications, Surrey, 1998

Nolan, William F., *Phil Hill: Yankee Champion*, Brown Fox Books, California, 1990

Nye, Doug, *Dino: The Little Ferrari*, Osprey, London, 1979

Orefici, Oscar, *Carlo Chiti: The Roaring Sinfonia*, Autocritica Edizione, Rome, 1991

Sheldon, Paul and D. Rabagliatti, *A Record of Grand Prix and Voiturette Racing 1960–1964*, St Leonard's Press, Shipley, 1985

Tanner, Hans and D. Nye, *Ferrari*, (6th edn), Haynes Publishing, Somerset, 1984

Yates, Brock, *Enzo Ferrari: The Man and Machine*, Bantam Books, London, 1992

JOURNALS

(Dates specified in text)

Autocar   *Cavallino*   *Forza*   *Motorsport*

Autosport   *Ferrari World*   *Motor Racing*   *Road and Track*

THE RECORD OF THE FERRARI 156 'SHARKNOSE'

1961

Date	Venue	Event	Chassis No.	Eng. Type	Driver	Result
25/4/61	Siracusa	Syracuse GP (nc)	0008	65 degree	G. Baghetti	1st
14/5/61	Monaco	Monaco GP	0001	120 degree	R. Ginther	2nd
			0003	65 degree	P. Hill	3rd
			0002	65 degree	W. von Trips	4th
14/5/61	Posillippo	Naples GP (nc)	0008	65 degree	G. Baghetti	1st
22/5/61	Zandvoort	Dutch GP	0004	120 degree	W. von Trips	1st
			0003	120 degree	P. Hill	2nd
			0001	120 degree	R. Ginther	5th
18/6/61	Spa	Belgian GP	0003	120 degree	P. Hill	1st
			0004	120 degree	W. von Trips	2nd
			0001	120 degree	R. Ginther	3rd
			0002	65 degree	O. Gendebein	4th
2/7/61	Rheims	French GP	0008	65 degree	G. Baghetti	1st
			0003	120 degree	P.Hill	9th
			0001	120 degree	R. Ginther	15th ret.
			0004	120 degree	W. von Trips	ret.
15/7/01	Aintree	British GP	0004	120 degree	W. von Trips	1st
			0003	120 degree	P. Hill	2nd
			0001	120 degree	R. Ginther	3rd
			0002	65 degree	G. Baghetti	ret.
8/8/61	Nürburgring	German GP	0004	120 degree	W. von Trips	2nd
			0003	120 degree	P. Hill	3rd
			0001	120 degree	R. Ginther	8th
			0002	65 degree	W. Mairesse	ret.
10/9/61	Monza	Italian GP	0002	120 degree	P. Hill	1st
			0001	120 degree	R. Ginther	ret.
			0003	120 degree	G. Baghetti	ret.
			0006	65 degree	R. Rodriguez	ret.
			0004	120 degree	W. von Trips (chassis destroyed)	crash

1962

Date	Venue	Event	Chassis No.	Eng. Type	Driver	Result
1/4/62	Heysel	Brussels GP (nc)	0006	65 degree	W. Mairesse	1st
23/4/62	Pau	Pau GP (nc)	0003	120 degree	R. Rodriguez	2nd
			0006	65 degree	L. Bandini	5th
28/4/62	Aintree	Aintree 200 (nc)	0007	120 degree	P. Hill	3rd
			0001	120 degree	G. Baghetti	4th
12/5/62	Silverstone	International Trophy (nc)	0001	120 degree	I. Ireland	4th
20/5/62	Posillippo	Naples GP (nc)	0001	120 degree	W. Mairesse	1st
			0006	65 degree	L. Bandini	2nd
20/5/62	Zandvoort	Dutch GP	0004[1]	120 degree	P. Hill	3rd
			0007	120 degree	G. Baghetti	4th
			0003	120 degree	R. Rodriguez	ret.
3/6/62	Monaco	Monaco GP	0007	120 degree	P. Hill	2nd
			0001	120 degree	L. Bandini	3rd
			0004[2]	120 degree	W. Mairesse	7th
			0004	120 degree	R. Rodriguez	nq
			0006	65 degree	R. Rodriguez	practice only
			0009	120 degree	P. Hill	practice only
17/6/62	Spa	Belgian GP	0009	120 degree	P. Hill	3rd
			0007[3]	120 degree	R. Rodriguez	4th
			0004[4]	120 degree	W. Mairesse (chassis destroyed)	crash
			0001[5]	120 degree	G. Baghetti	ret.
21/7/62	Aintree	British GP	0007	120 degree	P. Hill	ret.
5/8/62	Nürburgring	German GP	0006	65 degree	R. Rodriguez	6th
			0001	120 degree	G. Baghetti	10th
			0007[6]	120 degree	P. Hill	ret.
			0008[7]	120 degree	L. Bandini	ret.
19/8/62	Enna	Mediterranean GP (nc)	0009	120 degree	L. Bandini	1st
			0003	120 degree	G. Baghetti	2nd
16/9/62	Monza	Italian GP	0008/156/62/P	120 degree	W. Mairesse	4th
			0003	120 degree	G. Baghetti	5th
			0006	65 degree	L. Bandini	8th
			0002	120 degree	P. Hill	11th
			0007	120 degree	R. Rodriguez	14th ret.

nc = non-championship race   nq = not qualified

Notes:
1 May have been 0004/62 or 0002   2 May have been 0004/62 or 0002   3 May have been 1962 chassis 0003   4 As 2
5 May have been 1962 chassis 0001   6 Listed in entry by Ferrari as 0002   7 A non-'sharknose' 156/62/P

INDEX